Teach Yourself®

Set Up a Successful Small Business

Vera Hughes and David Weller

For UK order enquiries: please contact Bookpoint Ltd, 130 Milton Park, Abingdon, Oxon OX14 4SB. Telephone: +44 (0) 1235 827720. Fax: +44 (0) 1235 400454. Lines are open 09.00–17.00, Monday to Saturday, with a 24-hour message answering service. Details about our titles and how to order are available at www.teachyourself.com

Long renowned as the authoritative source for self-guided learning – with more than 50 million copies sold worldwide – the **Teach Yourself** series includes over 500 titles in the fields of languages, crafts, hobbies, business, computing and education.

British Library Cataloguing in Publication Data: a catalogue record for this title is available from the British Library.

This edition published 2010.

Previously published as *Teach Yourself Setting Up a Small Business*.

The **Teach Yourself** name is a registered trade mark of Hodder Headline.

Copyright © 2010 Vera Hughes and David Weller

Typeset by MPS Limited, A Macmillan Company.

Printed in Great Britain for Hodder Education, an Hachette UK Company, 338 Euston Road, London NW1 3BH, by CPI Cox & Wyman, Reading, Berkshire RG1 8EX.

The publisher has used its best endeavours to ensure that the URLs for external websites referred to in this book are correct and active at the time of going to press. However, the publisher and the author have no responsibility for the websites and can make no guarantee that a site will remain live or that the content will remain relevant, decent or appropriate.

Hachette UK's policy is to use papers that are natural, renewable and recyclable products and made from wood grown in sustainable forests. The logging and manufacturing processes are expected to conform to the environmental regulations of the country of origin.

Impression number   10 9 8 7 6 5 4
Year   2014 2013 2012 2011

Contents

Personal introduction

We started our own business DEVA Training Services in 1980. Before that we were involved in the retail industry for many years, David being the Training Manager for a widespread supermarket chain. Vera became Senior Training Adviser with the Manpower Services Commission specializing in office and retail training.

Redundancy gave us the push to start out on our own, training in a wide variety of organizations, so we have an extensive knowledge of the business world. We run our business as a partnership experiencing all the rewards and traumas of setting up and running a very small business.

In 1999 we set up Chester House Productions, our own theatre production company. We have a product (theatre presentations) which has to be written, learnt, rehearsed and performed. It has to be staged, with furniture, props and costumes. We have to know and attract our customers, mainly small clubs and societies. We have to market our product, through display boards, flyers, mailshots and our website. We have to keep our records, do the books and eventually pay our taxes. We do all this ourselves, so we know in depth and in detail what setting up and running a small business really means.

Like every other business, Chester House Productions has its peaks and troughs, its difficulties (fortunately very few) and its triumphs. Over the last ten years we have performed to over 15,000 people, and are still going strong. We hope you enjoy your own business as much as we enjoy ours. Please visit our website: www.chesterhouse.net.

Vera and David

Only got a minute?

Thinking of starting your own business? Just under way with your own business and wondering what to do next? These are the things you will need to consider to get your business up and running.

First of all, are you the sort of person who can run their own business? Not everybody can. Then, does your business meet a market need? You should do a customer profile and check on your competitors to make sure your product or service will sell.

You cannot run a business without some knowledge of business finance: how to cost your product or service, making a business plan and having sufficient finance to make sure your working capital and cash flow are under control.

Will you be working from home, or will you need to rent premises? And what sort of method of trading would best suit you? A partnership? Limited company? Network marketing or a franchise perhaps.

Then marketing. Customers need to know that you exist and what you have to offer. You need, too, to be able to sell yourself and your product or service to your customers.

Of course you have to do the books, see to your annual returns and eventually pay your taxes. A good accountant is a friend for life. This all ties in with business and personal finance and how to organize this. In all cases you will need an office of some sort.

Maybe you will need to employ others, even if only one part-time assistant. You will need to know and put into operation all the rules about employing other people. Opening a shop or an eating establishment are specialist areas, as are import, export and e-commerce.

Finally you need to know who to contact for help and advice and what 'the professionals' and various government and local authority agencies can do for you.

Good luck with your new enterprise!

5 Only got five minutes?

If you are just thinking of setting up your own business, or perhaps have just started it and are wondering what to do next, this short summary of the things you will need to know and do will help you on your way.

Are you the right type of person to be self-employed? Not everyone is. You will need motivation, organizational ability, time management skills, personal health and fitness and good communication skills. Then you will need to know whether your product or service will meet a market need. Study your competitors, make your own customer profile and, if possible, do a pilot scheme to make sure what you are offering actually works well for the customers you have in mind. A limited amount of market research will help you refine these ideas. Organizations such as Business Link are very helpful in these early stages.

Business finance will obviously be a very important part of your working life. How much will you charge for your product or service? A survey of your competitors on the internet will help you establish this, but you should also know how to calculate mark up and margin, and what the difference is. You may need some working capital to set up your business, and there are various avenues to explore, including bank loans and various grants. You will almost certainly need to make a business plan, and once you have been trading for a little while, will need to make and use a cash flow forecast. Cash flow problems are one of the main causes of business failure, even in large international organizations.

What about premises? Will you be able to work from home, or will you need to rent premises? A shop or workshop perhaps, not forgetting office and storage space for raw materials and products ready for delivery. Consultants such as management or

HR consultants or trainers can often work from home. In all cases the premises must be fit for the purpose.

Next, what method of trading will best suit you and your business? Sole trader, partnership, limited partnership, limited company? Or perhaps franchising or network marketing, or even a registered charity. Each method of trading has its own merits, with rules about making annual returns and other accounting aspects.

Customers and clients need to know you exist, so marketing is a very important part of any business. For some, advertising and mailshots are appropriate. For others brochures, flyers and leaflets are a must. For all publicity materials you will need to think about design, layout, production and distribution, always bearing in mind the image you want to convey about yourself and your product or service. Networking is an excellent way to market your small business, so you will probably find it beneficial to join business clubs. Marketing means keeping your name at the front of your customers' or clients' minds.

Selling a service is different from selling a product in many ways, but you still need good selling skills to get your message across. You will need to think about how to prepare, how to approach customers or clients, how to establish their needs and the difference between features and benefits. You will need to be able to deal with objections and how to close the sale. Finally you might be able to sell up or sell on – those additional sales and services.

Inevitably you will have to do the books, keeping track of all your receipts and payments, petty cash, banking procedures and, very often, VAT returns. These arise sooner than you think, as your business expands. You will need to keep records of your customers and your sales, so that you know what sells well and what doesn't, and adapt accordingly. Will your system be done manually or on computer? Probably the latter, particularly if you employ others, or have many business transactions to account for. If this is not one of your great strengths, you might consider employing a book-keeper, who will keep your records and returns straight throughout the year. At the year end you will have to account for your trading for the past year, and this is where a good accountant is essential.

All this ties in with personal and business finance. How will you be paid, personally, for your contribution to the business? What about your National Insurance payments and pension provision? HM Revenue & Customs will need to know your tax situation. What, for example, should be recorded as fees or takings, and what are legitimate business expenses?

You may well need the help and advice of the professionals, and where to find them. Depending on your business, you may need the services of accountants, architects, banks and building societies, estate agents, HM Revenue & Customs, insurance brokers, printers, office services and solicitors.

You will certainly need your own office space somewhere, even if it is the corner of your dining table to begin with. You will need office stationery and know what to include in documents such as invoices, estimates, quotations and statements. Your email and, sometimes, letter communication must continue to reflect your image and be accurate and well laid out. Office equipment will include a desktop and/or laptop, phones and a photocopier. Then there is The Health and Safety at Work etc. Act 1974.

If you employ other people, even if it is only one part-time assistant, you will need to know and put into effect all the rules about employing others, which is where a good book-keeper can certainly help. You will need to consider staff recruitment, wages and salaries, particulars of employment, insurance and, again HASAWA (The Health and Safety at Work etc. Act 1974). The Data Protection Act will also apply to your business.

If you are opening a shop or an eating establishment, there are many additional things to consider. For example, would your premises be better in a town centre, or on the periphery, and what shape of premises will best suit your business? You have to think what image you want to portray and the people you need to work with you. Of course there is stocktaking to be done, and many things to do with taking money and banking it to consider. Security will be a high priority, and so will complying with various legal requirements. Once you are ready, you will need to advertise your grand opening.

Your business may need to import goods, so you will need to know how to deal with suppliers not based in the UK. What documentation will you need, and how about customs and transportation? Insurance is an important part of all this. You may not at first be into exporting, unless you develop an e-commerce business, when you will be sending goods worldwide.

E-commerce is an exciting form of trading, but, as in any other business, you need to know what you are doing. Starting in a small way by buying and selling small items yourself, perhaps on eBay, can be a good way to start. Then you can progress to opening an eBay shop or creating your own website, which must be attractive, accurate and easy to use. You will need to take good photos of your products and describe them succinctly, and this takes a long time. How will your customers pay for your products, and what is your policy on returns, damage and so on? A professional website designer may be a great help to you.

Running your own business can be exciting and rewarding, but it can also be stressful and exhausting. The unwavering support of your family is essential, as is your ability to balance home and business life. You will need very good planning skills, particularly if children and other dependants are involved. Your health is an important part of your life – you literally cannot afford to be ill, so you must take steps to eat and exercise sensibly. Good health also helps with your appearance and the personal image you project. You will certainly need plenty of energy. In most cases your business and personal finances should be kept separate, so that other adult members of your household know where they stand. Running a home and a business is not an easy thing to do.

Finally you need to know where to go for help and advice when you need it. As well as the professionals, there are many extremely useful websites especially those run by government departments. Make the most of your networking opportunities such as your Chamber of Commerce, breakfast and other business clubs, and the Federation of Small Businesses. Business Link is an invaluable source of advice and information, specially set up to help small businesses. Your local authorities can also be a helpful source, often facilitating short courses and sometimes providing funding. And don't forget your local college, particularly if you need certain qualifications such as a First Aid Certificate.

This summary can only give you an overview of all the many business aspects you will need to consider. Each chapter contains details to guide you along the way, with checklists to encourage you to check that you have done everything you should do.

Good luck with your new enterprise!

Acknowledgements

The authors gratefully acknowledge the help and expertise of the following people: Tony Adams, Accountant, on all matters to do with accountancy; Brenda Locke of Datacounts, on book-keeping and internet banking; Gillian Leach, Solicitor and Partner in Blake Lapthorn Linnell, on all matters to do with employing others; Linda Lewis of Chic Intérieur, on import and export matters; Larch Gauld of Virtual Support Services, on website, website design and maintenance.

1

The first step

In this chapter:
- *Is it saleable? A sound product or service; the market need; suppliers*
- *Can you sell it? Personal attributes required; self-motivation; organizational ability; management of time; energy and health; communication skills; pilot scheme*

The first thing anyone needs before setting up any kind of business is an idea, or perhaps more precisely the idea of starting in business at all. It sometimes happens in a blinding flash, but more than likely it insinuates itself and gradually the idea of setting up a business develops until it is hard to remember when it was not there.

Before the idea takes over too much, certain questions need to be asked in order to keep things realistic and in proportion – not to kill off the idea, but rather to have a controlled development of it.

Talking to a neutral business adviser could be a sound way of doing this. For example, good Business Link managers say that the most important part of their counselling work for potential business start-ups lies in dissuading people from investing their life savings and re-mortgaging their houses for a business idea that is flawed and will never succeed. The majority of people who get as far as going to their local Business Link for advice turn up with ideas that could spell disaster for them if the ideas are not at least adapted significantly and they are often abandoned. Of those who go ahead and launch businesses, many will fail within three years (30 per cent according to the Department for Business,

Innovation & Skills' statistics), and only a small minority will actually grow. So while not wishing to put a damper on things from the start, it is only fair to point out how important it is not to get carried away with an idea just because you want to believe in it. Ask an objective business counsellor to assess the idea before you sink your money and your family's security into it.

Insight

Contact your local Business Link for objective advice. They helped us with our broadband application.

Is it saleable?

A SOUND PRODUCT OR SERVICE

The first question to ask about your idea could take the following form: What precisely is the product or service I am going to offer? followed by the key question: Why should customers buy MY product or service rather than those which exist already?

Insight

If you are not honest with yourself, you might get the answer you want, not the right answer.

There is a distinct advantage if the product you are intending to offer is a legal requirement, in the sense that, potentially, you have a captive market. Items related to health and safety, for example, fire extinguishers or even Fire Exit and other related statutory signs would come into this category. You can probably think of other areas which could apply.

Nevertheless that key question still needs to be answered, and answered realistically: Why should customers buy MY product or service rather than those which exist already? Make a list of the good points about your product – they could form the basis of your marketing strategy.

THE MARKET NEED

Continue to question your idea:

▶ *How many people are likely to want to buy my product or service?*
▶ *Will the numbers be sufficient to justify proceeding with the idea?*
▶ *What competition already exists?*
▶ *How well established is it?*
▶ *Will I be able to compete?*
▶ *Is there a particular segment which I could concentrate on?*
▶ *Is what I am considering generally an expanding or a contracting market?*
▶ *Will I be infringing, even inadvertently, other people's intellectual property rights? Is your idea really your own, or are you copying someone else's? Visit the Patent Office website, www.patent.gov.uk.*

The finding of the answers to these and other related questions forms the basis of the market research exercise which is necessary at this early stage to turn a hunch or idea into something more down-to-earth and practical, or to confirm that the original idea is sound.

Insight

If you are using questionnaires, allow people to be anonymous if they wish. If people want to add their name, they'll always find somewhere to write it.

As a small trader or partnership, you cannot afford to embark on a very large market research exercise, but it is worthwhile trying to establish whether what sells well to friends and colleagues, or business contacts, will be bought by others.

You can research the market in an informal way by asking friends, family and colleagues what they think of your idea. A more businesslike approach is to send out or give out a short questionnaire. You could do this at networking meetings, on-line, or with gatherings of family or friends. Expect a better response if you hand out the questionnaires personally and get people to complete them then and there.

Whichever method of distribution you choose, design your questionnaire carefully, taking these guidelines into account:

▶ *One A4 sheet at most, or computer equivalent*
▶ *Ask questions which require tick box responses, people don't like to write long answers*
▶ *If you ask people to rate an attribute of your product/service, give them an even number of boxes to tick – four or six. If you give them five they are likely to go down the middle*
▶ *Leave space for additional comments*
▶ *Don't ask for a lot of personal information. You might be infringing the Data Protection Act – refer to www.dataprotection.gov.uk*
▶ *Make giving their name optional. People often give 'truer' answers if they know they are anonymous*
▶ *Draw up a good system for analysing the responses.*

Insight

Use your networking contacts to do some market research, your local Business Clubs, for example.

Your local Business Link runs market research courses for people starting up in business. Ask at your Job Centre, your local Business Link or your local college to see what courses are available. The courses include not only market research, but marketing, book-keeping, selling and many other matters dealt with in this book. A book can give you useful general guidelines – a course tutor can give you personal attention and expertise. 'Taking it further' includes typical courses run by Business Links.

SUPPLIERS

If your business idea involves selling a product, you will need to obtain either the raw materials which you are going to transform into something else, or the components which will create your finished article.

These items will need to be obtained from suitable suppliers. You will find that there is no shortage of people wanting to sell you things for your business. What you must do is draw up your product specifications very carefully and decide on the suppliers (it is probably better to have more than one source) who will provide that quantity and the quality you need at the price you wish to pay.

Insight
Search the web – it's the only place we could find collarless shirts and stiff collars!

Make a list of the components you need, and for each component write down the potential suppliers, their prices, delivery dates, settlement terms and product quality. Making such a list helps you to think clearly and objectively.

Can you sell it?

PERSONAL ATTRIBUTES REQUIRED

The personal attribute most required is belief in the product or service you are about to sell. If you do not have absolute faith in your product or the quality of your service, you will never get your business off the ground.

You must try not to be put off if other people's reactions do not initially match your enthusiasm.

SELF-MOTIVATION

The belief in your product or service is the first step in self-motivation; what follows depends on your own ability to move off the starting line and keep up the momentum.

Sometimes people feel that those who have their own businesses are lucky, because they can suit themselves whether they work or not. To a certain extent this is true, of course: if you decide one morning that you would rather stay in bed than turn out in the cold to sell your product or service, that is up to you – your competitors will be delighted!

Self-motivation is an attitude of mind as much as anything, and your attitude must at all times be to develop your business. If you are a sole trader this can be more difficult, since you may not have anyone else to help you with your motivational process. So self-motivation should perhaps be coupled with self-discipline. Determine to set yourself a regular business routine, and do all you can to keep to it. As you achieve this regular routine, you will find that your self-motivation improves dramatically. There is nothing like a successful meeting or telephone call to stimulate motivation – the hard work is the initial effort needed to arrange that meeting or make that telephone call in the first place.

ORGANIZATIONAL ABILITY

An absolute requirement of anyone who starts a new business is the ability to operate in an organized way. You cannot work effectively in a muddle.

This has nothing to do with the workshop with wood shavings on the floor, or even the desk with papers strewn over it. This is the ability to know when and where the next appointment is, of having a system to pick up messages periodically, of dealing with correspondence quickly and efficiently, of being able to put your hand on specific pieces of information promptly and responding effectively to queries or enquiries.

This is all part of self-discipline which, as we have just seen, is also part of that all-important self-motivation.

MANAGEMENT OF TIME

Whether you are the chairperson of an international business organization or a sole trader, the amount of time available to you is exactly the same: there are precisely 24 hours in the day for both parties.

How those 24 hours are utilized is where the differences arise. Chairs of multi-nationals probably have other people around them to ease the pressure on their time, while the sole trader more than likely has no such luxury, or at best very limited help. The management of available time effectively is therefore significant, requiring, once again, a high degree of self-discipline.

One of the greatest causes of the mis-management of time is the very human one of doing those things which we want to do. You can always find a valid reason for putting off the unpleasant job.

Consider the following checklist – select those which are your most important ones now:

---

50 time management guidelines: for people setting up their own business

PLANNING

1 *Plan your time; do not let it control you*
2 *Assess your work – projects, tasks, etc. – and allocate priorities*
3 *Arrange and allocate your priorities into categories A, B, C and D*
4 *Throw away the Ds*
5 *Keep the Cs to be read during non-priority time*

6 *Date and/or time check the Bs: they are usually important but not urgent*

7 *Sub-prioritize your As – A1, A2, A3, etc.*

8 *Do the A1s now, then your other As – not those attractive Cs!*

9 *Chop the big task down into smaller, more manageable pieces*

10 *Estimate the finishing time for a task, not just the starting time*

11 *Always ask the questions: What? Who? Where? Why? When? How?*

OPERATING

12 *Use the 'To Do' system*

13 *Have a daily 'To Do' list – particularly for your A items*

Insight

On your TO DO list, write down and cross off a job you have just done – it's a wonderful motivator!

14 *Review your daily list, first thing in the morning or last thing in the evening, and plan your priorities*

15 *Keep your daily 'To Do' list always in sight*

16 *As you clear each item, delete it in brilliant red – just looking at a list of completed tasks makes you feel even better!*

17 *Do not include too many items – remember the jobs which always crop up unexpectedly*

18 *Maintain a second 'To Do' list for longer-term tasks or those to which a date cannot yet be given*

19 *Transfer items from the second list to the daily list whenever relevant*

20 *Use the 'To Do' lists, do not ignore them – they are probably your most powerful time management tools*

21 *Write it down: do not try to keep your 'To Do' lists in your head – keep that free for actually doing them!*

22 *Leave some time for the unexpected*

23 *Have the things you need constantly to hand in one place*

24 *Identify and concentrate on the high-yield tasks if you have the choice*

TELEPHONE CONTROL

25 *Master your telephone techniques*

26 *Plan your telephone calls: use telephone 'To Do' lists as telephone agendas*

27 *If possible, arrange a specific 'call back' time – do not just say 'I'll ring you later' or, even worse, 'You ring me later'*

28 *If interrupted during a task by a telephone call, before answering pencil in your next thoughts. When you return to your task you will know what you were going to do or say next*

29 *Cross-index your telephone directory: name as one entry, organization as the other*

30 *Quickly get to the purpose of the call: it is pleasant to socialize (gossip?), but it wastes a lot of time*

31 *Make sure you get the call-back name and number correctly: do not hesitate to ask for information until you have got it right*

DISCIPLINE

32 *Time management is 99 per cent self-discipline*

33 *Do the unpleasant task first, or as early as possible, particularly if it is your A1. It is most people's experience that these tasks usually turn out to be less unpleasant than was anticipated*

34 *Use the recommended time management techniques: they have been proved to work*

35 *Learn to say 'No'*

36 *Make sure you do it right first time: every time you have to re-try, you are wasting time*

37 *Avoid procrastination: get on with it*

38 *Set yourself personal deadlines for most tasks and stick to them if at all possible*

39 *Stick to the task you know must be done*

40 *Do one thing at a time*

41 *Always have something to do: even if it is constructive relaxation*

42 *Always be on time yourself*

43 *Handle paper only once if at all possible*

44 *Read only what you must: the rest can be read in your C time*

TRAVELLING

45 *Do not leave it until the last minute to set off*
46 *Do not be a one-side-of-the-town-to-the-other traveller: plan groups of visits within easy range of each other*
47 *Use car cassette or CD learning*
48 *Use waiting time to make mobile phone calls*
49 *Use train time to: read, write, brainstorm ideas with yourself*

SUMMARY

50 *Plan what you have to do, how it is going to be done, where it is to be done, by when it has to be done. Why has it to be done at all?*

From 'Training and Development' April 1988,
in an article by Leslie Rae FITD

Consider this checklist against the prime purpose of this section, *Can You Sell It?* If a sensible use of this checklist creates more selling time for you, then you will be getting your priorities right.

Everything you do should contribute to your self-improvement and thereby the improvement of your business. So use this checklist at regular intervals to review your progress and assess how much you have achieved – you will probably be pleasantly surprised.

ENERGY AND HEALTH

The show must go on, as we who work in the theatre know well. The show certainly must go on as far as a small business is concerned, especially for the sole trader, since there is no one else to 'perform'.

In setting up a new business, the energy and health of the participants is something which should receive serious consideration, since a lot of energy is going to be needed in those all-important early stages.

For example, if prior to setting up your own business you received, as part of your employment package, an annual health checkup, it is well worth considering continuing with this. Ask yourself whether you can afford to be ill in your new business situation, and whether the fee for an annual checkup is a worthwhile expense, not to say investment in the most valuable asset your business has – you and your health.

There are many ways in which this can be done. It is worthwhile sorting out your arrangements at this early stage, before the pressures begin taking their toll.

If you are going to be selling your goods or services face to face with your prospective customers, you will need to be well on top of the task. In order to be alert and able to respond to the situation of the moment, you will need to have at least reasonable health.

Insight
Use exercise time (treadmill, running etc.) or car time to do some planning in your head. We use these times to 'do lines' for our performances.

You will find a lot of this initial activity both physically and mentally taxing, and you will need to be able to start each new day with a certain amount of zeal and enthusiasm. Even if you have been used to doing this sort of work before, the pressure of having your name 'over the door' adds an extra incentive to – and is a drain on – your energy resources.

COMMUNICATION SKILLS

In order to sell something, whether it is a product or a service, a certain degree of skill in communication is required. The actual process of selling is covered in detail in Chapter 6, but there are other methods of communication which are relevant in business.

Spoken

Spoken communication does not only apply to the selling situation, but is necessary for discussions with all sorts of people – potential customers, suppliers, reps, professional advisers, etc. These can be either face to face or via the telephone. The ability to be fluent and comprehensible, particularly on the telephone, is a skill to be developed.

> **Insight**
>
> If you are texting, rather than speaking, make sure the person you are texting understands your text language.

One way of doing this is to record yourself – if possible making a real telephone call. When listening to it afterwards, do not think in general terms of how good and bad it is, but try to analyse:

- ▶ *whether all the words can be clearly heard*
- ▶ *whether you say a lot of 'ums' and 'ers'*
- ▶ *whether you repeat yourself too much*
- ▶ *whether your voice sounds pleasant and friendly (try smiling down the phone).*

You need not be afraid of recording the other person, because that voice will not be heard on your tape.

> **Insight**
>
> Do you know how to get rid of 'chatters' on a business phone call? It's easy. You do three things. First, stand up. It makes you sound more authoritative. Next, summarize, yet again if necessary, what has been agreed between you. Then thank the caller and end the call. Try it – it works!

Written

Written communication is necessary in a number of areas – emails, letters, estimates, quotations, invoices, etc. Your business communications must go out without spelling, grammar and punctuation mistakes. If you know you are weak in this area, use the services of someone who knows what they are doing. You will probably not have the time at this stage to improve your own English language skills. If you only need to brush up on your written English, try *English Language Skills* by Vera Hughes, published by Greenwich Exchange.

Presentation of written communication is almost as important as the content, because the way written material is laid out reflects your business image. This is covered in Chapter 10.

PILOT SCHEME

Before committing yourself too deeply to your prospective business, it is quite a good idea to 'test the water'. If it is possible, create a sample batch of your product, and embark on a selling exercise to test the reaction of potential buyers or outlets.

Try to gather as much useful information as possible during this exercise – pluses and minuses, assessing the strengths and weaknesses of what you have to offer, and the way in which you are presenting it.

To do this exercise when you are offering a service is a little more difficult, since what you have to offer is not as tangible as an actual product. Perhaps you could offer to provide a sample of your service at a very advantageous price in order to test the response of potential clients. The *Marketing your own consultancy* section of Chapter 5 might be helpful to you in this situation.

Insight

If you're still in employment, it's worth doing a pilot scheme at evenings and weekends, in case you need to keep going with the day job.

Getting your business off the ground will often take a lot longer than you thought. There is a great deal to do in the early stages, and sometimes there are delays beyond your control. To minimize delay, invest time at these very early stages in learning how to do the research, the marketing and the selling in the most time- and cost-effective way.

CHECKLIST

▶ *Make a list of the reasons why people should want to buy your product or service.*

▶ *Carry out some market research – seek help from your local Business Link and/or college.*

▶ *Make a list of potential suppliers and their strong points.*

▶ *Rate yourself on a 1–10 scale for the following:*
   ▷ *Motivation*
   ▷ *Organizational ability*
   ▷ *Management of time*
   ▷ *Fitness*
   ▷ *Communication skills*
   Decide what needs improving, and plan how to improve it.

▶ *Run a pilot scheme.*

2

Business finance

In this chapter:

- *Costing the product or service: cost price; mark-up and margin; selling price*
- *Working capital and cash flow*
- *Making a business plan*
- *Presenting your case for funding: banks; other sources of funding*

Costing the product or service

COST PRICE

Insight

You're in business to make a profit.

The costs of a business can be sub-divided into several categories, which will have an effect on arriving at the cost price of the product or service, either directly or indirectly.

Examples of costs are:

Labour   Direct workers: those directly involved in handling goods
Indirect workers: administration, support services and maintenance
In the small business one person could well be involved in both categories

Machinery and materials	Components: goods and machines used to produce the finished product
Interest	Charges on borrowing: loans e.g. overdrafts
Overheads	Light, heat, rent, rates, telephone, travelling, postage, internet, etc.
Taxes	National Insurance, VAT, HM Revenue & Customs, etc.

Portions of these various costs need to be taken into account when arriving at the cost price of your product.

The same should be done if you are offering a service. What you are selling is your time, and you have to work out the value of that, while taking account of the costs of the business.

Insight

When developing a new project, we list, as we go along, the cost of everything to do with that production, (e.g. wigs and whiskers, costumes etc.), including petty cash items such as dye (for dyeing spats!).

MARK-UP AND MARGIN

A business exists to make a profit: your business will exist only if it makes a profit. This profit is generally expressed in one of two ways – as a percentage of either the cost price or the selling price.

If based on the cost price it is referred to as **mark-up**, and can be expressed as follows:

$$\frac{\text{Selling Price} - \text{Cost Price}}{\text{Cost Price}} \times 100$$

An example calculation:

$$\frac{£20.00 - £15.00}{£15.00} = \frac{5}{15} \times 100$$

$$= \frac{500}{15} = 33\tfrac{1}{3}\%$$

If based on the selling price it is referred to as **margin**, and can be expressed as follows:

$$\frac{\text{Selling Price} - \text{Cost Price}}{\text{Selling Price}} \times 100$$

An example calculation:

$$\frac{£20.00 - £15.00}{£20.00} = \frac{5}{20} \times 100$$

$$= \frac{500}{20} = 25\%$$

Mark-up is always greater (in percentage terms) than margin, although the monetary figure is the same. It is vital, if discussing profit percentages, to establish whether the figures being quoted are mark-up or margin – confusion can follow if this is not done.

Mark-up and margins can very easily be worked out on a calculator with a $\boxed{\%}$ key, probably along these lines:

Mark-up   SP − CP
               Answer ÷ CP
               $\boxed{\%}$ key = $x\%$
Margin   SP − CP
               Answer ÷ SP
               $\boxed{\%}$ key = $x\%$

Insight

The 'pile it high and sell it cheap' businesses will have a small profit margin. Niche business margins will be much greater.

SELLING PRICE

The selling price should provide a suitable margin between that and the cost price to produce a profit for the business. It must also reflect the market in which you trade. Find out what other people charge for a similar product or service. The profit must be adequate and continuous, and cover current expenses, while providing a balance for the future.

Insight
Use the net to find out what your competitors charge. Pretend you are a customer.

Working capital and cash flow

Working capital is the value of the current assets of the business less the current liabilities.

Assets	These are what the business owns, and can be divided into two broad categories:
	Fixed assets – land and buildings, machinery, motor vehicles, etc.
	Current assets – debtors, stock, cash in hand, cash at bank, etc.
Liabilities	These are what are owed to others, and again can be divided into two broad categories:
	Long-term liabilities – capital introduced, bank loans, etc.
	Current liabilities – creditors, overdraft, wages and salaries, etc.

A business should never allow itself to run short of working capital, which should always be sufficient to finance the running of the business. Lack of working capital is a very common reason for business failure: it means, for example, that creditors cannot be paid, or advantage taken of special offers from suppliers. Working capital ratio can be calculated as follows:

$$\frac{\text{Current Assets}}{\text{Current Liabilities}}$$

Although the ratio of 1:1 is the minimum working capital ratio, a business should endeavour to improve on this, and doing the calculation from time to time is a useful exercise. A business needs cash to be profitable, and has to ensure that the flow of cash does not dry up.

Obtaining a large order seems good news to a small business, but take care that the extra expense involved, particularly that of obtaining the materials necessary to fulfil the work, does not reduce the available cash to an unacceptable level – remember that the overheads and other fixed expenses still have to be met.

How can a business ensure that a sudden need for cash does not become a burden? One way is to try to keep abreast of the current financial situation. A bank statement will give an indication, albeit in hindsight, although a visit to the cash dispenser at the bank will give you the real up-to-date position. Beware, though, of acting on the figure displayed by the cash dispenser, because there might be some cheques which are as yet uncleared, or some regular payments which have not yet been deducted from the balance. Always keep your records of money due and received up to date in a Cash Book. This will give a true picture of how you stand financially. Telephone or internet banking are very good for giving up-to-the-minute information.

A method of establishing this on a more formalized basis is to draw up a Cash Flow Forecast, which will enable you to keep the up-to-date position constantly before you, and help to make the right decision when the unexpected turns up.

Insight

One of the main causes of the collapse of world-renowned banks was cash flow problems. You should be able to manage your business better than that!

A Cash Flow Forecast should be drawn up, manually or electronically, for a 12-month period, although it could be done for a month or a quarter. Each month should show the Budget figures with space next to them for the Actual figures to be inserted. Here is a rough pattern:

CASH FLOW FORECAST				
Month	January		February	
	BUDGET	ACTUAL	BUDGET	ACTUAL
Opening balance INCOMING – Sales – Other	–		–	
A Total receipts				
OUTGOING – Materials – Light/Heat – Rent/Rates – Wages/Salaries – Telephone/Postage etc.				
B Total payments				
A–B Balance (+ or –)				
CLOSING BALANCE (Transferred to next month)				

Take appropriate action when A–B Balance varies from the Budget figure. Keep new work within the cash resources available.

Turn down work if necessary to prevent cash flow problems – remember that a sale does not necessarily mean immediate payment; allow for delays in getting your money.

Make certain that the business never owes more than can be met by the current balance plus, if necessary, the value of any assets which could be sold. Try to show a sensible and realistic projected profit – one that is not too high or too low for your type of business.

Making a Business Plan

Producing a Business Plan will not automatically ensure that your business will be successful, but it will help you to face the future in a realistic way and, very important, present your business ideas to somebody else in a formal and factual manner.

The way in which the plan is drawn up and presented is important. The business which takes the trouble to produce its Business Plan in a logical and presentable way is more than likely to adopt the same approach to its business opportunities.

Visit the major banks and collect their booklets on business planning. You will find many helpful suggestions on how to draw up a Business Plan. It might be a wise move to base yours on the format suggested by the bank you intend to approach with your Business Plan!

Do not be afraid to seek assistance in drawing up your Business Plan, but beware of copying other people's. Your plan concerns your business and your business alone; your accountant or Business Link can provide invaluable help in this task. It is not a job to be rushed; careful preparation stands a better chance of success than a document hurriedly thrown together. In any case keep it simple and to the point.

The headings you could consider for your Business Plan are:

Purpose of business	What you are going to sell, and broadly, in what sort of market
Marketing strategy	Based on market research and carefully costed
Competition	Where you fit in and where you differ
Starting up requirements	Premises, machinery, materials, furniture, vehicles, telecommunications, desktop etc.
Grey areas of the business	The unknown, points where you cannot yet be precise
The way forward	Some idea of how long it will take to get your business really up and running
The people in your business	Detail their qualifications (if appropriate and their expertise and experience, including your own

End on an optimistic and enthusiastic note.

Presenting your case for funding

BANKS

Banks want to lend you money: it is a vital part of their business, but, of course, they want to be certain that your business is a suitable one with which to be involved.

It is worth doing a little research before approaching a bank. Do not just go to your local branch because it is the nearest. Banks tend to specialize in different areas; find out from people in a similar business which banks are likely to look favourably on your business.

For example, if you are setting up a business in the entertainment industry, you might stand the chance of getting a more sympathetic hearing if you take your Business Plan for producing a series of promotional videos to a bank in the West End of London rather than one in the West Country. The London bank will be more used to dealing with that type of business, and would appreciate the nature of the risks involved.

A preliminary chat to see whether a bank is prepared to lend money to you at all is a good idea, and may save you time. If the answer is definitely 'No', you know where you stand.

When you have obtained your appointment, make sure you have everything ready. You need a well-presented Business Plan and Cash Flow Forecast.

Draw up a detailed list of:

- ▶ *what you want the money for*
- ▶ *how you intend to pay it back.*

Remember to include the interest on the loan in your calculations.

It is better to ask for a long-term loan, so try to get as long a pay-back period as you can. It is always possible to pay back a loan early, but not always so easy to extend the loan if your business is not doing as well as you hoped.

Try to anticipate the questions you are likely to be asked. It would probably be sensible to arrange for your accountant to attend with you. In any case try to have a 'dry run' where you can state the main facts of your case and reassure yourself that you can do this with confidence.

OTHER SOURCES OF FUNDING

Insight

Parents will, when they can, sometimes make their adult children an interest-free loan. Make sure an agreement is drawn up in a business-like manner – and stick to it.

Banks are not the only lenders of money, but a bank is a good start for up to £50,000. Above that figure you could consider a building society, an insurance company or a merchant bank. You could also consider topping up your mortgage to introduce capital into your business. You could also approach your local authority or one of the government departments (DWP). If you are between 14 and 30 you could apply to The Prince's Trust (www.princes-trust.org.uk), well known for giving financial and practical support to young people. Likewise, if you are over 50, try Prime, a registered charity linked to Age Concern (www.primeinitiative.org.uk). Ask your accountant to advise you on sources of funding, where to go for the best deal and how best to present your request for a loan.

Insight

We got a grant for connecting to broadband from our County Council, from attending a free internet one-day seminar put on by our local Council and run by Business Link.

Conclusion

Many small businesses do not fully understand the role that business planning can play in helping them to develop their business and maximize their resources. Many mistakenly believe that a Business Plan is just an aid to secure finance, rather than an essential business practice which can increase the overall efficiency of a business.

CHECKLIST

▶ *How much will it cost to produce your product?*
  or
  How much will it cost to render your service (including your time)?

▶ *What sort of profit margin will you expect to get?*

▶ *What will be the selling price of your product or service?*

▶ *How will you ensure that you have enough working capital and cashflow?*

▶ *Have you done your Cash Flow Forecast?*

▶ *Have you done your Business Plan?*

▶ *If you need funding, have you detailed what you need and how you are going to pay it back?*

3

....

Premises

In this chapter:
- **Working from home**
- **Workshops, warehouses and factories**
- **Office premises**
- **Finding out what is available**
- **Support and grants**
- **NB For retail outlets see Chapter 12**

Working from home

For some people, working from home is out of the question, because of manufacturing processes, storage space required, for instance, but for many it can be a good starting point. The types of business which are suitable for working from home are likely to be:

- ▶ *consultancy*
- ▶ *teaching/training*
- ▶ *'cottage' industry (e.g. crafts, food)*
- ▶ *professions (e.g. accountants, therapists, architects).*

Sometimes a good business address is essential to your image; in this case an obviously residential address would be a handicap.

CUSTOMER AND CLIENT ACCESS

If yours is the type of business where you go to your clients or customers – goods made at home and delivered or services rendered on other people's premises perhaps – a home base could work quite well.

It is essential that your customers are able to get in touch with you quickly and easily, by phone, fax or email at times convenient to them. You also have to guard your own privacy, however, and make it clear that business is to be done in business hours, whatever those may be. For example, if your business hours exclude mornings, and you work afternoons, evenings and weekends, this must be made clear to your customers. Home hairdressing could be an example here.

If your business requires your customers to come to you, if only occasionally (consultants or accountants, for instance) it is very important to be able to receive them in a business-like atmosphere, with all the privacy they would expect from business premises. Parking should be convenient, if possible, and the entry to your home easy and pleasant. Being greeted by a doorbell which does not work, a barking dog and a noisy child is not a good introduction to a business atmosphere.

If you are doing business with customers in your home, a separate office or study is highly desirable.

SPACE

If your business is a cottage industry, you obviously need enough space in which to process what you are making. A shed or garage can sometimes be used. Remember that you will also need storage space for:

- ▶ *equipment*
- ▶ *materials, including wrapping or packing materials*
- ▶ *tools*
- ▶ *items ready for delivery to customers.*

and good access for getting these things in and out of your home without causing annoyance to the rest of your household or your neighbours.

You will also need space for the office side of the business (see Chapter 10). Equipment such as photocopiers and desktops takes up quite a bit of room, and is often difficult to move because of size or access to power points. Laptops are more manoeuvrable and mobile phones take up very little space. A separate office is ideal, if possible.

Insight

We need space to store our scenery and costumes, and we have a separate 'office'. Our double garage makes a good rehearsal space.

If you are supplying a service, as opposed to a product, from your home, less space is needed, but you still need to be able to store paper, files, office machinery and so on. Take account of this, and try to keep your business space and your private space separate.

ROUTINE

It is important to set yourself some sort of routine for working from home. You do not have the discipline of leaving for another place of work, and it is very easy to get sidetracked.

Working from home means that you do not spend time travelling to work, but you have to be strict about the time you therefore save. If you decide to set this time aside for personal matters, that is your decision and one of the benefits of being self-employed and working from home.

It is easy to get distracted by:

▶ *external noises (lawn mower, traffic)*
▶ *internal noises (animals, children, TV, radio).*

It is also easy to be interrupted by:

▶ *callers (meter reader, delivery vans)*
▶ *visitors*
▶ *family and friends*

▶ *personal phone calls*
▶ *domestic chores (cooking, cleaning, shopping, fetching children from school, etc.)*

People tend to think that because you are at home you are not working. If you can establish a routine for your work it will help your own discipline and that of other people. You need to come to an agreement with other members of the household about who does what, when and where. If you have been used to working in an office or a factory, you will find it quite difficult to adapt to the routine of working at or from home, and you should make allowances for this adjustment period.

OVERHEADS

You need to be clear, as soon as possible, what proportion of the overheads on your home you can claim for business purposes. You should be able to claim a proportion of your:

▶ *lighting and heating*
▶ *telephone*
▶ *security*
▶ *cleaning.*

Reckon on being able to claim anything to do with the business, not with the house. If you start claiming for rates or water rates, you may be liable to Capital Gains Tax when you sell the house. The Council Tax should not be affected at all by the fact that you work from home.

Insight

Be careful to use office and storage spaces for other purposes as well as business, otherwise you could be liable to Capital Gains Tax when you sell the property.

Check with your accountant what proportion of household expenses can be deemed to be for business use and how this should be recorded in the books (Chapter 7). For example, you should be able to claim VAT (if you are VAT registered) on your business telephone calls, and on a proportion of any telephone rental charges.

If you have cleaning help in the home some of this payment might be offset as a business expense, but take care that your cleaning person does not become an employee for personal tax or National Insurance (NI) purposes.

Other things you might be able to claim for are a guard dog, installing security devices, extra telephone points and secretarial services by other members of the household, but check with your accountant first.

You need to be sure, when setting up your business at home, that you are not altering the use of the property or part of it from residential to light industrial. Check with the local authority byelaws and a solicitor who is fully conversant with these.

ADVANTAGES AND DISADVANTAGES OF WORKING FROM HOME

Advantages	Disadvantages
▶ cheaper	▶ distractions and interruptions
▶ no travelling	▶ lack of space
▶ can help with domestic finances	▶ lack of business address
▶ flexibility	▶ lack of business atmosphere

Workshops, warehouses and factories

If you are dealing with products, as opposed to services, you will often need to rent premises in which to work. Premises available can range from small workshops of no more than 500 sq ft (50 sq m) to small factories, depending on requirements. It is unusual for someone starting out in business to need a large factory straight away, but it is possible.

A warehouse is normally used for storage purposes only – storage of materials before processing, storage of deliveries ready for despatch or storage if you are the middle person between the seller and the buyer.

SIZE

The size depends on what you are producing, the size of the machinery or equipment you use and the amount of space needed for immediate storage of materials, packaging, wrapping and the finished product ready for despatch. It is sometimes more cost-effective to rent a slightly larger workshop which will accommodate all these requirements comfortably than to rent a separate storage area or warehouse.

When calculating the size required, remember to allow adequate space for the people who are going to work there, for facilities for those people (personal belongings storage, refreshments and so on) and for a certain amount of office space. Even if you are doing the books elsewhere (at home, for example) you will need a space on site for processing paperwork; this space will need to house a desktop or laptop. You will probably need somewhere to put a landline.

ACCESS

You need easy access to your premises for:

▶ *yourself*
▶ *your staff*
▶ *deliveries*
▶ *despatch.*

Make sure that you can get in to your premises when you want to – 24 hours if necessary. Make sure that your staff can get in if you are not there for any reason.

Consider access for large delivery vehicles, particularly if you buy in bulk. What unloading facilities are there?

Insight

We always need to take scenery, costumes etc. with us in one or two estate cars. For a new production we do a trial loading, making diagrams of what fits where, if necessary.

Is there adequate parking for you, your staff and your own vehicle(s) for despatching goods? What are the loading facilities for your own vehicles? Are lifts available if necessary?

Try making a list of all the people and products which will be going in and out of the premises and check for each whether they can get in and out in a cost-effective and practical way.

SECURITY

What security measures are in force to protect the premises you are going to rent? If you have 24-hour access, who else does? How secure are the windows and doors? How secure will your merchandise or products be while being unloaded and loaded? What lighting arrangements are there? What security system will you be allowed to install, if you need to? What security arrangements can be made for personal belongings?

Insight

It's very distressing and time-consuming to have things stolen on a personal level, but when it concerns your business, and consequently your livelihood, it's even more alarming. Do you always lock your vehicle when you leave it?

Check the security:

- ▶ *outside the premises*
- ▶ *inside the premises*
- ▶ *when receiving deliveries*
- ▶ *when despatching deliveries*

- *of personal property and vehicles*
- *of company vehicles.*

HEALTH AND SAFETY

Make sure you are aware of the provisions of the Health and Safety at Work etc. Act 1974 (HASAWA) and its subsequent workplace regulations. Check:

- *COSHH Regulations 1989 (Control of Substances Hazardous to Health)*
- *machine guards and rules and regulations for cleaning and maintenance*
- *fire exits*
- *fire appliances*
- *evacuation procedures*
- *protective clothing, if necessary.*

If you are an employer, you are responsible for providing safe and healthy working conditions for your staff (see Chapter 11). The Health and Safety Executive (HSE) publishes many leaflets and books, several of which are free. (Telephone 0845 3450055 or www.hse.gov.uk.)

If your workshop, factory or warehouse is part of an industrial complex, you need to check the health and safety regulations relating to that complex, and that you are able to comply with them.

Insight

In some cases staff under 18 may use machines, but not clean them, because it means taking them apart. If you have an apprentice or young person working for you, remember to check this.

Remember to check the safety of your company vehicles and to have them regularly serviced, particularly if they are driven by someone other than yourself.

COST

It is impossible to suggest a fair rent for premises because this varies so widely in different parts of the country, and often in different parts of the same town.

It is helpful to make a list of what is **essential** to you when searching for premises and what is **desirable**. Also, considering your Cash Flow Forecast (see Chapter 2, pages 20–21), set a maximum rent you are prepared to pay, and stick to it. Remember you might have to pay a one-off premium, sometimes returnable at the termination of the tenancy, as well as rent in advance when you agree to rent the premises.

Insight

We save a lot of money by not having to rent rehearsal space. We can rehearse at any time of the day or night!

Check whether the rent quoted is inclusive or exclusive of such items as rates, communal services (security guard, window cleaner, for instance), building maintenance and so on. Are there any hidden extras?

It is not always the cheapest rent which is the most economical. Balance your needs against your preferences; if the property does not meet the essentials you require, go elsewhere: be prepared to pay a bit more if necessary, but not beyond the maximum you have set yourself.

Office premises

If you are offering a service, it might not be appropriate to work from home because of lack of space. Perhaps you are in partnership, and it would not be sensible to work from the home of either or any of the partners. In these cases you will be looking for office accommodation to rent.

Much of what was said under *Workshops, Warehouses and Factories* applies here. You need to consider:

- ▶ *what size you need*
- ▶ *access to your office*
- ▶ *security*
- ▶ *health and safety and*
- ▶ *cost.*

There are, however, additional matters to be considered when renting office accommodation.

IMAGE

A good address and prestigious offices are vital to some businesses. For example, an interior design consultancy needs an address and office premises and furniture in keeping with its up-market image. It is worth looking in areas that are being gentrified as well as those that are well established as prestige areas. If you can get in early in an area which is about to move up-market, so much the better.

Again it will depend on whether clients come to you or you go to them, but it is unusual for your offices never to be visited by potential clients, whatever your business. Therefore you need offices into which you will not be ashamed to welcome visitors, without going into unnecessary expense. This is tied up with the next section on *Services*.

SERVICES

Sometimes office accommodation comes with certain services, such as cleaning, window cleaning, reception, switchboard, fax, mail in and out. You should check which of these services is included in the rent, if any.

When visiting the premises, if it is an office block of which you intend to rent one small part, note how well the reception area is maintained, whether the grass (if any) is cut, whether the plants are tended and how well you are received by the Receptionist. These are all indicative of how well the building is run and this is an indication of the image that will be conveyed to your own clients.

If you are planning to rent premises above shops, visit during the busiest time of the day so that you can judge the noise levels or smells from neighbouring premises to see whether they are acceptable.

ACCOMMODATION

When calculating the square footage of accommodation you require, remember to take account of the provisions of the Offices, Shops and Railway Premises Act 1963, which lays down, among other things, how much working space each person should have, and what toilet facilities should be available.

Look for adequate power points for your office machinery and desk lamps, and check that the temperature can be regulated so that it is not too cold for the people nor too hot for the equipment.

Office workers normally require either good car parking facilities or easy access to shops and public transport.

Finding out what is available

The main sources of information about what is available in the way of business premises to rent are:

- *estate agents who specialize in that type of property*
- *local authorities, for premises owned and rented by them*
- *your local library*
- *Business Links*
- *your own observations.*

LIBRARIES

If your local library is a good one – that is, it offers an up-to-date
reference section and knowledgeable staff – you have a highly
prized source of information. It can supply you with copies of:

- *specialist books on finding premises*
- *lists of professional advisers*
- *lists of premises available*
- *publications on how to choose and rent premises*
- *the Land Registers which show publicly owned land which is
  underutilized*
- *the Business Location Handbook by area in the UK*
- *enterprise or development zones, planning offices, etc.*

ESTATE AGENTS

The library will probably have a list of estate agents which specialize
in business premises. Local business directories are helpful.

An agent with local knowledge is an advantage. Test by asking
about a property of which you have personal knowledge to see
what the agent has to say about it.

Insight

Your local networking clubs or societies can usually engage
speakers, especially from local authorities, who know about
the business opportunities and grants available in your area.

BUSINESS LINKS

One of your most useful sources of help, support and advice is
your local Business Link. These are government-funded bodies
which aim to be a link between business and providers of support,
courses, etc. such as local colleges, professionals (solicitors,
bankers, etc.) and training providers. They are especially good for
someone starting up their own business, with free advice, often free
training events and an instructive website. See 'Taking it further'

for a list of typical courses. Your library will be able to give you the contact number for your local Business Link.

LOCAL AUTHORITIES

Local authorities often own large areas of property and are prepared to rent office and manufacturing accommodation to small businesses. They also hold records of planning applications, so that you can look up where developments are likely to occur and therefore where premises are likely to be available. They will also have details of business parks and industrial estates. The local telephone directory will normally give some indication of the correct department to approach.

YOUR OWN OBSERVATION

Keep a look-out yourself for likely empty premises. Look above shops and in basements, particularly for office accommodation. Nearby shops and offices will often know who the landlord is.

Watch for signs of private and public developments – premises gutted, new access roads being built. A property which is being run down might be a good short-term bet for you, because terms are likely to be favourable.

Support and grants

This section is about government and local authority support for renting premises. It is difficult to be precise about this, because government policy changes and the funds available from local authorities fluctuate.

As a rule of thumb, areas which government and local authorities want to promote, such as areas of high unemployment or deserted factories, are more likely than areas which are booming to offer support to growing businesses.

Support is more likely to come in the form of subsidies for premises to rent than as direct grants, although grants are sometimes available for setting up specific projects – new technology, for example. These grants tend to go to the larger enterprises, but if you are embarking on a business which is either in the right geographical area or of the right type, it is worth making enquiries. The Department for Business, Innovation & Skills (BIS) has the information. Some businesses can get funding from the EU (European Union). Your Business Link will be able to advise you on this.

CHECKLIST

▶ *Make a list of what is essential and what is desirable.*

▶ *Decide whether to work from home or not.*

▶ *When renting workshop, warehouse, factory or office accommodation consider:*
  ▷ *Size*
  ▷ *Access*
  ▷ *Security*
  ▷ *Health and safety*
  ▷ *Image*
  ▷ *Services*
  ▷ *Cost: set a maximum you can afford, and stick to it*

▶ *To find out what is available use:*
  ▷ *Local authorities*
  ▷ *Estate agents*
  ▷ *Libraries*
  ▷ *Business Links*
  ▷ *Your own observation*

▶ *For government and local authority support, consult:*
  ▷ *Department for Business, Innovation & Skills (Tel: 0207 215 5000; www.bis.gov.uk)*
  ▷ *Local authority (number in The Phone Book)*

4

Methods of trading

In this chapter:
- **Sole trader**
- **Partnership**
- **Limited company**
- **Limited partnership**
- **Franchise**
- **Registered charity**
- **Multi-level marketing**

Sole trader

If you are a one-person business, perhaps working from home, probably the best method of trading is as a sole trader. You do not need to register with any official body, but you do need some stationery with your name and business address (see Chapter 10). You should also have a document displayed in your office showing the name and address of your business and its proprietor(s). You need to inform HM Revenue & Customs and the Department of Work and Pensions (DWP) that you are self-employed and if your **turnover** (that is, the amount of money you actually take in sales in a financial year) is £68,000 or more (2009 figures) you need to be VAT registered (see Chapter 7 and Chapter 9). This figure may change each year. It is surprising how quickly your turnover will reach this figure.

If you are trading under your own name – for instance, 'John Robinson Associates', or 'J. Robinson' or something very similar – you do not need to check whether someone else is trading under the same name. If you choose to trade under a name which is quite different from yours (for example, 'Parisian Photos'), check with your solicitor that there are no legal objections to your doing so. Your own name and address must still appear on your stationery.

As a sole trader you are personally responsible for all your business transactions. This means that your personal income, from whatever source, your house, your car and even your estate after your death can be used to pay off debts. Some people make sure that the house is at least in joint names and that other possessions (such as the car) are registered in the name of another member of the family. Check with your solicitor the best way of covering yourself. You do not have to have your accounts audited, but it is as well to employ an accountant who specializes in very small businesses to prepare your annual accounts and tax returns for HM Revenue & Customs purposes (see Chapter 9).

Partnership

If two or more of you are working together in the business, you can trade as a partnership. Like a sole trader, you do not have to register your business, but you do have to:

▶ *show your names and address on your stationery*
▶ *inform HM Revenue & Customs and the DWP that you are self-employed*
▶ *check that any name under which you choose to trade is legally acceptable*
▶ *register for VAT if your turnover exceeds £68,000 per year (2009 figures).*

All the partners are collectively and individually liable for the debts of the business. This includes any business debts of any of the partners, even if you do not know that these debts have been incurred.

You are not required by law to draw up a Partnership Agreement, but it is wise to do this, setting out all the conditions under which you have agreed to enter into business together. A solicitor specializing in small businesses and partnerships will be able to advise you.

> **Insight**
>
> We have always traded as a partnership, being careful to keep our business and personal activities and finances separate.

The partnership ceases instantly upon the death of any of the partners, so it is wise to take out life insurance on each partner so that the remaining partner(s) have enough money to continue trading if they want to. The deceased partner's share of the business becomes part of his or her personal estate.

As with a sole trader, you do not have to have your accounts audited, but it is wise to employ an accountant for HM Revenue & Customs purposes.

> **Insight**
>
> We have never, as two partners, analysed whether one earns more than another in any one week, month or year. More partnerships break up over money squabbles than for any other causes.

Limited company

Many small businesses choose to set themselves up as a limited company. The big advantage of this method of trading is that your business liability is limited to the business, and you would not be required to pay debts out of your personal moneys, except in the case of fraud.

A limited company can have only one shareholder who could act as director and company secretary, and the company must be registered with the Companies Registration Office (CRO), Companies House, Crown Way, Maindy, Cardiff CF14 3UZ. Telephone their Contacts Centre on 0870 3333636 or visit their website www.companieshouse.gov.uk.

The Company's stationery, including its emails, must show its name and address and place and number of registration. The fact that it is 'limited' must appear somewhere on the paper – either in the company name or as a separate statement. The stationery must also show the names (first name or initials plus surname) of either all the directors or none of them.

The accounts must be properly audited by a registered auditor within ten months of the end of the company's financial year and filed annually at the CRO, so that anyone, particularly shareholders who are not directors of the company, can inspect them if they wish. The accountant is usually appointed at the first Annual General Meeting and continues as auditor as long as both parties wish.

Insight

As well as auditing your accounts, a good accountant can save you a substantial amount of tax, quite legitimately.

Very small companies may not have to file annual accounts because of the Totally Exempt Companies System. Ask your accountant's advice.

You raise capital by selling shares in the company to the directors and others. The chair of the company, if one is appointed, is normally responsible to the shareholders.

The outline of the company's trading purposes and methods is drawn up in the Memorandum and Articles of Association (often known as Mem and Arts). The Memorandum outlines the purpose of the company (its overall strategy) and the Articles of Association outline the way in which it will work – number of

directors, voting rights and so on (the company tactics).
These documents need to be drawn up carefully; you should
employ a solicitor.

You can buy a ready-made limited company 'off-the-shelf' from
a company registration agent, with its Mem and Arts already
prepared; virtually all you need to do is fill in the names of the
director(s) and secretary and the company's proposed address,
and pay the appropriate fee. You need to be sure that any such
business meets your own requirements.

You can, of course, buy a business which already exists,
including its goodwill, so that you can start trading straight
away. In this case you need to look very carefully at its
accounts, because they can be deceptive (without any intention
to deceive). Employ an accountant for this; it is false economy
not to do so.

Limited partnership

A limited partnership (LLP) combines the flexibility and status of
a partnership with limited liability for its members. The potential
liability of a member is limited to the amount that the member has
agreed to contribute to the partnership if the LLP goes into liquidation.

The LLP is required to submit annual accounts to Companies
House, and if necessary have them audited by a qualified
accountant, unless small business exemption applies; ask your
accountant about this. Companies House must also be notified of
any changes in partners and particulars, just as if the LLP were a
limited company.

Franchise

This has become a very popular way of starting up in business, and can be a sensible way of doing so, because you can profit from the know-how of the franchisor (you would be the franchisee). Some very well-known companies run a franchise – household names like Cartridge World, GreenThumb UK, Kall Kwik, Prontaprint and Thorntons, to name a few. Opportunities are available in at least 30 different industry sectors. The Franchise World Directory gives details of all available franchise businesses. See 'Taking it further' for contact details.

Insight

It's interesting, when walking down your local High Street, to note how many well-known names are franchises.

The *advantages* of becoming a franchisee are:

▶ *You are trading under a well-known name*
▶ *You receive initial and ongoing advice and training in, for example, merchandising, stock control, buying, employing staff, book-keeping, etc.*
▶ *Franchisors often have a special arrangement with a bank and/or key suppliers for getting start-up money (see Chapter 2), which can reduce the burden of franchise fees*
▶ *You are part of nationwide advertising*
▶ *Sometimes the franchisor will find suitable premises and will lease or mortgage the premises to the franchisee.*

Disadvantages are:

▶ *You have to pay a franchise fee*
▶ *You would have to pay an ongoing management fee – probably between 5% and 7% of the turnover*
▶ *The start-up capital can be quite large – up to £500,000 – but can be as low as £5,000. However, depending on your credit*

rating and the standing of the franchisor, banks could advance up to 50–60%

▶ *In most networks you have to stick strictly to the systems laid down by the franchisor so freedom to trade in the manner in which you wish to trade can be limited.*

There are two main types of franchise for the small business:

▶ *Retailing in a wide variety of fashionable shops and eating establishments: income depends on the profits made*

▶ *Rendering a service, such as carpet cleaning or car tuning: income often depends on the number of hours worked.*

The British Franchise Association (telephone 01491 578050) is also a good source of information. Its website address is www.thebfa.org.uk. Another good source of help is *Get Started in Franchising* by Kurt Illetschko.

Registered charity

Tax advantages are likely to be available to a charity: generally most charities are exempt from income tax, corporation tax and capital gains tax. A charity which wishes to reclaim tax will need to register with HM Revenue & Customs Charities (IR Charities). Some supplies to charities are specifically exempted from VAT.

HM Revenue & Customs Charities gives information about tax reliefs and tax obligations (including VAT) at www.hmrc.gov.uk/charities/index.htm. There are a number of 'Help Sheets' available at www.hmrc.gov.uk/charities/leaflets.htm on issues such as trading, fund raising, stamp duty and giving to charities. You can also make enquiries by telephone, email or post. See the website for current contact details.

It is a fairly complicated matter to register as a charity so seek advice from your solicitor.

English legislation states that to qualify as a charity, an organization will have to be only for charitable purposes (see the list below) *and* be for the public benefit. To benefit the public, a charity must benefit either the community as a whole, or a significant portion of it. An organization that is mainly for the benefit of one or more named individuals is unlikely to meet the public benefit test.

Insight

Some arts organizations register as charities, because they work with schools or disadvantaged sections of the community, as well as carrying out their main function. Chester House Productions could not do this; we are in business to make a profit for ourselves.

A purpose is charitable if it falls within one or more of the following heads:

▶ *the prevention of relief or poverty*
▶ *the advancement of education*
▶ *the advancement of religion*
▶ *the advancement of health or the saving of lives*
▶ *the advancement of citizenship or community development*
▶ *the advancement of the arts, culture, heritage or science*
▶ *the advancement of amateur sport*
▶ *the advancement of human rights, conflict resolution or reconciliation, or the promotion of religious or racial harmony or equality and diversity*
▶ *the advancement of environmental protection or improvement*
▶ *the relief of those in need by reason of youth, age, ill-health, disability, financial hardship or other disadvantage*
▶ *the advancement of animal welfare*
▶ *the promotion of the efficiency of the armed forces of the Crown.*

Arrangements in Scotland, Northern Ireland and possibly Wales are different. Visit their websites.

Multi-level marketing

This is a very specialized method of trading sometimes called
network marketing. Multi-level marketing is not illegal, and can
make quite substantial income for those who wish to employ this
trading method. It is a respectable development from pyramid
selling, which got itself a bad name in the 1960s.

> **Insight**
> Network marketing is often used by individuals selling
> clothing, jewellery, beauty products etc. This method of
> trading can fit in very well with home commitments.

HOW DOES IT WORK?

You join a trading scheme as a 'participant' and buy goods or
services from the person or people running the scheme, or from
other participants. You then sell these goods or services to the
general public in their homes.

You make a profit on the difference between the cost (buying) price
and the selling price and usually by other rewards such as:

▶ *bonuses for recruiting new participants*
▶ *commission on sales of your products made by other
  participants*
▶ *higher bonuses or commission if you are promoted to a higher
  level in the scheme*
▶ *payments for providing services (e.g. training) to other
  participants.*

You need to be good at selling things and/or recruiting other
participants if you are to make a substantial income from this type
of scheme.

There are very strict rules for multi-level marketing companies.
Visit the BIS website at www.bis.gov.uk.

Multi-level marketing can be a profitable way of doing business, but you need to beware of illegal schemes, or getting caught up in a legal scheme without fully realizing its implications.

Insight

One essential: you must believe absolutely in the product you are selling. Have you ever tried persuading someone to go along with something you don't believe in? It's almost impossible.

CHECKLIST

▶ **Sole trader:**
  ▷ *One-person business*
  ▷ *No registration requirement*
  ▷ *Headed stationery*
  ▷ *Inform HM Revenue & Customs and DWP*
  ▷ *Personally liable*

▶ **Partnership:**
  ▷ *Two or more partners*
  ▷ *No registration required*
  ▷ *Headed stationery*
  ▷ *All partners liable for debts, apart from tax*
  ▷ *Partnership ceases on death of one partner*
  ▷ *Partnership Agreement desirable*

▶ **Limited company:**
  ▷ *Liability limited to the business*
  ▷ *Must register with Companies Registration Office (telephone 0870 3333636)*
  ▷ *Accounts must be audited by qualified accountant*
  ▷ *Headed stationery must show address, registration number and 'limited'. All directors' names or none*
  ▷ *Memorandum and Articles of Association required*

▶ **Limited partnership:**
  ▷ *Flexibility and status of partnership*
  ▷ *Limited liability*
  ▷ *Registration, annual accounts and name changes to Companies House*

▶ **Franchise:**
  ▷ *Advantages: well-known name; advice and training; help with funding; sometimes help with premises*
  ▷ *Disadvantages: franchise fee; ongoing management fee; limited freedom in trading practice*

- ▷ *Information from The British Franchise Association (www.thebfa.org.uk; telephone 01491 578050)*

▶ **Registered charity:**
  - ▷ *Many tax advantages*
  - ▷ *Strict rules to follow*
  - ▷ *Must have charitable purposes*
  - ▷ *Must negotiate with Charity Commissioners*
  - ▷ *Suitable for arts organizations*

▶ **Multi-level marketing:**
  - ▷ *Become a 'participant' in a scheme*
  - ▷ *Buy from other participants or from central distribution*
  - ▷ *Sell to other participants or general public*
  - ▷ *Expected to recruit other participants*
  - ▷ *Strict rules to follow*
  - ▷ *Beware illegal schemes*

5

Marketing

In this chapter:
- *Your marketing profile*
- *Marketing methods: advertisements; mailshots; mailshots by email or fax; leaflet drops; printing and artwork requirements; leads and personal contacts; trade shows and exhibitions; your website*
- *Marketing your own consultancy*
- *Image*

Your marketing profile

Having decided on the product or service your business is going to be offering, it is important to invest time in deciding how this product or service is going to be presented in the most effective way – your marketing profile.

Ask yourself questions to define precisely what the business is all about. The actual answer will vary considerably of course, depending on the type of business involved, but in general terms this could be a pattern to follow:

Insight

Chester House Productions has quite a narrow marketing profile. Our customers are mainly clubs and societies on the speaking circuit, with the occasional small festival. Our customers are happy to sit and listen.

What are we selling?

- ▶ *A product, a service, a skill?*

Who will be our customers?

- ▶ *Will they be regulars who will keep coming back to us?*
- ▶ *Will they be casual passers-by?*
- ▶ *Will they be trade, who will then sell on our product to others?*
- ▶ *Will they be the end users of our product?*

Who will be the actual buyer of our product or service?

- ▶ *Particularly in large organizations, who will be the decision-maker?*

What will our customers actually need?

- ▶ *Will our basic product/service be sufficient?*
- ▶ *Will there be opportunities for selling 'extras'?*

Where is our market?

- ▶ *What is the likely demand for what we are offering?*
- ▶ *What is the size of the existing market?*
- ▶ *What is our potential share likely to be?*
- ▶ *What is likely to be the spending power of potential customers?*

What is the competition?

- ▶ *How intense is the competition?*
- ▶ *Who are they?*
- ▶ *How well do they meet the needs of their customers?*
- ▶ *Are there areas of weakness which provide opportunities for our business?*

From these generalities, try to draw up a precise self-questioning checklist for your business. A lot of wasted time and money, the possible result if a product or service is presented in a rather arbitrary way, can be avoided by such an analysis.

Marketing methods

You need to let people know that your business exists, what you have to offer and how your customers could benefit from using its products or services. This is the aim of marketing.

There are various methods of marketing which are available to a business. Some are more suitable than others, so part of the secret of successful marketing is using those methods which are likely to be the most effective.

> **Insight**
> Pick up other people's marketing material, or note which adverts in the local papers stand out. Then analyse what is good about them.

ADVERTISEMENTS

Very broadly, advertisements – and advertising generally – can be divided into two categories, selective and non-selective.

With *selective* advertisements you will be aiming your material at particular groups or categories of potential customer, which you have previously identified. This identification could well be one of the results of your self-questioning exercise (see page 55) – which makes the time spent on that task even more worthwhile.

One advantage of selective advertising is that you can be very precise in your material, perhaps even to the extent of incorporating a modest jargon word or two, since your target audience will understand. It might also create a (subconscious) impression on the readers that you know what you are talking about – which, of course, you do.

Non-selective advertising on the other hand, by its very nature, must be more general in its approach, striking a balance between being too basic or elementary for those in the know, and inviting the person who is unfamiliar with the subject matter to find out more.

This leads us neatly into the well-used advertising formula AIDA – which is particularly applicable to non-selective advertising, for what AIDA aims to do, through the advertising material, is to:

▶ *gain the Attention of the reader*
▶ *hold the Interest of the reader*
▶ *create a Desire in the reader for your product or service*
▶ *stimulate Action in the reader to BUY.*

which, after all, is the sole purpose of advertisements. It is the route toward this target which needs careful planning.

Insight

For general, non-specific adverts, do those you have picked up or studied follow the AIDA plan?

Advertisements cost money: ineffective advertisements waste money. There are three main sources of expense involved in advertisements: firstly, the design and layout of your message; secondly, the actual production of the advertisement and finally the distribution of the advertisement.

Design and layout
Even if you undertake this yourself, remember your time is money, so there is still an expense involved. It could be worth your while enlisting the help of someone who is knowledgeable in copywriting and layout. At the very least study the advertisements of businesses promoting a similar product or service to yours. Compile a scrapbook for easy reference – this could help you devise a design and layout of your own.

Production

This includes the expense of the actual printing process, and everything which leads up to that moment, like setting up the text, and producing plates.

You can get advertising material printed in several different ways, and of course the cost will vary. One of the best ways to get leaflets printed is to take a disk containing the final, formatted copy, or else camera-ready copy (CRC) printed on a high-resolution printer to your copyshop or print shop. Make sure your system and the printer's system are compatible.

Full-colour glossy brochures will need the advice and professionalism of an experienced printer, and will be more expensive. You should think about your company's image when deciding which is right for you.

Make a Difference with Your Marketing by J Jonathan Gabay is an excellent book on marketing in general.

One very useful tip at this stage – *always* proofread any advertising material; if possible get someone else to do it as well. This can save a lot of heartache when an error is discovered after the print run is completed.

Distribution

How distribution is carried out will depend on the form of the advertisement. If it is printed in a newspaper or magazine, the distribution will be controlled by the circulation of the publication.

If it is your business or service you are advertising, as distinct from the products, the advertisement will take a different form. Perhaps a display advertisement in a local paper or *Yellow Pages* or other local directory.

For information on advertising in *Yellow Pages* ring 0800 60 50 60. They will advise you on advertising in *Yellow Pages* itself,

Business Pages, *Talking Pages* and *Yell.com*. Thomson offer similar advertising services and can be contacted on 01252 555555 or www.thomsonlocal.com for details of local contacts.

Mailshots

Being on the receiving end of mailshots, one could be forgiven for thinking that they are the most effective form of advertising known, since everyone seems to use them. But consider for a moment how many you, personally, have responded to; probably only a very few. This is the big minus for this form of advertising – the response rate is traditionally low, and yet it remains a much used method.

As with advertisements, mailshots can be selective or non-selective. Unless you intend to send mailshots in very large numbers, it would be advisable to use selective mailshots to specified target groups. This could be approached in several ways, for instance alphabetical, geographical. Try to compile as big a list as possible of organizations which might use your product or service. List the most obvious ones first, but do not be too rigid, particularly if you are offering products or services which have a more universal application. Think of organizations which, although they might be diverse in themselves, have a common need which is covered by your product or service. Ask yourself: how many products do I have and does this affect how many potential customers are available for my business?

When you have compiled your list, rather than tackle it all in one go, work though it piecemeal and select a manageable number: this will help you to regulate the time involved in preparation, follow up and evaluating the results. This does not mean to say that you only need to prepare the number of mailshots you actually plan to send out. If you have a period of time in which you can make up a large number of packs, by all means do so. You do not necessarily have to despatch them all at the same time.

As a rule of thumb, aim to send each mailshot to a named person. This may involve a telephone call to find out from a business who is responsible for your product or service.

Obtain:

- *the name and job title*
- *correct name of the company*
- *the full postal address.*

You cannot always rely on *Trade Directory* information, even in the current edition, because people move or change jobs and businesses get taken over; it is best to check.

Write to the 'big boys' on your list first, even if you feel there is not much hope because they have everything tied up already. If this turns out to be the case, at least you know for sure, but there again at that particular time they may be in the market to consider your product or service ...

The mailshot package itself will probably consist of a brochure or some other form of printed matter describing your product or service, together with a standard letter of introduction. Follow the KISS principle and Keep It Short and Simple. Do not be tempted to tell the recipients your whole story at this first encounter – but just enough for them to want to know more.

Try to keep your letter to one side of one sheet of headed paper. Follow this broad format: introduce yourself and your organization by stating who you are and what you are offering, and in effect ask 'Can we do business?' Indicate that you intend to follow up this written introduction with a telephone call.

In the letter, do not quote a precise time when you will ring (something may prevent you) or suggest a specific date for a meeting (you do not know the recipient's commitments), but wait until you telephone, when you will have a direct response to

a suggested date, and alternatives can be discussed – and resolved –
there and then.

Insight

Mailshot your regular customers regularly, based on your
customer database. One of the objectives of marketing is to
keep your name in your customers' minds. Use something
new or different as a reason to mailshot.

Set yourself a deadline, and some sort of timetable for your telephone
follow-up calls. Probably the best times, from the recipients' point
of view, are Tuesday to Thursday, preferably mornings if you can
make it. Monday mornings and Friday afternoons are probably best
avoided – the recipients are just getting their week underway on the
one, and thinking about going off on the other. There might well be
cases, of course, where these are the ideal times to telephone. You
will get to know your own type of business best.

Preparation for your follow-up telephone call will help it to be
effective. Compile a checklist of points to make. Try to avoid a
fully-written-out script. You can be thrown if the recipient does not
respond in the way you expect – or asks a question at the wrong time!

Your call could take this form, once you are connected to the right
person:

Identify yourself and your organization.
Ask whether your brochure has been received, to which the
answer will broadly be 'Yes' or 'No'.
If the answer is 'No', briefly explain the substance of your letter
and brochure in broad terms (having a copy of both in front of
you will prove invaluable in these circumstances).
Offer to send a further set.
At this stage, and if the answer to your original question was
'Yes', ask whether your kind of product or type of service is
being stocked or used at present. Again the answer will broadly
be 'Yes' or 'No'.
(Contd)

This is your cue to describe the benefits to that business of what you are offering; in the case of the 'No' answer you can start from basics; with the 'Yes' response, explain what is different about yours, and the benefits to that business of including your product or service in their existing range.

If at this stage there are discernible signs of interest, try to gain a definite commitment of some sort, e.g. a meeting, or even a sample order.

Be sure to confirm any arrangements in writing, and ensure that they are met in full.

If, however, the response is still negative, ask whether there is any possibility of reconsidering in the future, and whether you may ring again.

It might be worthwhile sending a letter thanking the individual for the conversation, and confirming that you will be in touch in a few months.

File the information for future reference – and mark your diary to remind you to make that call when the time comes around.

Insight

Give your mailshot letter a big, bold heading. Put your main selling points in one or more PSs. Readers glance first at the top of the letter, then the bottom.

MAILSHOTS BY EMAIL OR FAX

You are probably aware that, as a private individual, or as a business, you can register on the Telephone Preference Service (TPS) to avoid receiving cold call telephone calls. Similarly you can also avoid a great deal of junk mail being delivered to you.

As a business person yourself, you must be aware that you are not allowed to send unsolicited 'junk' faxes to private individuals. Also, if you try to send bulk emails, you may well find your Internet Service Provider (ISP – see *Your website* section below) 'spams out' your emails and even disables your account.

LEAFLET DROPS

Leaflets can be a very reasonable way of passing on your message to potential customers, particularly if those customers are the end users, and leaflets can be distributed directly into their homes via their letterboxes. As with mailshots, one must accept that the take-up rate can be low.

Insight

Use your own laptop or desktop, plus a good (really good) printer/photocopier to produce your own flyers or leaflets in colour. Use the best quality paper or thin card. This can be time-consuming, but means you can do a small print run as and when you need it. Chester House Productions produces all its own flyers and programmes this way.

This distribution could be done by hand, by post or even as inserts in special interest magazines.

The first method is obviously the cheapest. It is a job one could do oneself, or perhaps by cajoling members of the family into helping. Perhaps your friendly newsagent could be persuaded to allow the paperboys and girls to deliver your leaflets with (not in) the papers, to give a blanket, non-selective, coverage.

Post would involve more expense. A wider geographical area could be covered, especially if you were doing a selective distribution and trying to target the right type of firm or household. *Mailguide: A Comprehensive Guide to Royal Mail Services* is available at your local library or from FREEPOST, Royal London House, 22 Finsbury Square, London EC2A 1NL.

Inserting your leaflet into specialist publications could be another way of achieving a selective distribution – the cost might be comparable with that of a direct postal distribution, so could be worth looking into.

But what of the leaflet itself? Like the mailshot, there is only a short time to get your message across – between the letterbox and the waste bin! This means that the techniques you use in compiling your leaflet must gain the immediate attention of the recipient (AIDA applies in this situation, too), and be relevant to the product or service you want to sell – and do not forget, that is why you are doing the exercise.

Consider 'visual aids' to attract the attention of the person picking up your leaflet, and to underline your selling message. Drawings, photographs, cartoons could all come into this category – but choose with care, they must reflect the correct image of what you are offering. Do not infringe other people's copyright by using their material without permission.

Think about the actual material you will use for the leaflet: something suitable to the image, for instance plain paper or coloured paper? Glossy or matt finish? What sort of weight paper would be appropriate? Would thin card be going too far?

The size of the leaflet could be significant. Would A5 be too small or A4 too large? Will it be a flat sheet, or will it be folded? If so, how – in two or in three? (Who will do the folding and how long will it take? What would be the extra cost, and would it be worthwhile?)

Give any prices you quote on the leaflet a 'life', for example, 'Valid until end of June', 'Special offer for July only' or indicate a time span by implication – 'Spring 2010'.

Make any follow-up action easy: prepaid reply, freephone, credit card payment.

Leaflet drops could be a cost-effective way of testing the market with a business idea. As with the mailshot method, take a conscious look at the leaflets which you receive through your door or in the post, and use them as a yardstick to designing an effective one of your own.

PRINTING AND ARTWORK REQUIREMENTS

Pretty well all the things we have been considering in this chapter could involve printing and artwork in varying degrees.

This is an area in which it is worth doing a little research. There are many, many printers about, as a glance in your *Yellow Pages* or free press will show you. You need to find those who specialize in the type of work you want. Perhaps the printer who produces your stationery is not the right one to produce your mailshot or advertising leaflet.

Very likely the printers who produce advertising material will have their own people or contacts to produce suitable artwork.

You will very often find the name of the printer on pieces of advertising material you receive from other people. If the standard or style is the sort of thing you are looking for, a visit or a phone call might be profitable.

Printing can be expensive, so try to get things cut and dried before committing yourself. You should consider producing your own marketing material from your desktop and colour printer, but make sure they look professional.

LEADS AND PERSONAL CONTACTS

Personal contact can be a very valuable source of seeking business in the early days of trading, particularly among those who knew you in the business world before you set up your enterprise. Your name and reputation will still mean something – this will fade, of course, with the passing of time, and as you build up an identity under your own name.

Insight

We have found advertising to be our least successful marketing tool. We use flyers, a display board with good photographs and the occasional mailshot. Personal recommendation is our best form of advertising.

These personal contacts, if of no direct use to you, could be the means of pointing you towards others who could make use of your product or services. Utilize this method of introduction to the full in these critical early days, which could help you to establish a useful track record. Always have your business card handy to give to your personal contacts. Joining your local Chamber of Commerce or business club is a good way to network.

A word of thanks to the giver of a successful lead would no doubt be appreciated, and, who knows, others may be forthcoming!

TRADE SHOWS AND EXHIBITIONS

A small business will not normally want to take a stand at a large national or international trade show, which is expensive. However, you should consider attending local shows, agricultural fairs and smaller trade shows or exhibitions.

Visit these when you are planning your enterprise, to see if they would be suitable when you are ready for your launch or expansion. If your business is craft-based, you should aim to take part in these shows a couple of times a year. Trade magazines will tell you how to enter.

YOUR WEBSITE

Almost all businesses need a website, to be seen to be up-to-date and to display their products or services to sell, whether on-line or in some other way. A website increases the potential customer base enormously, allowing you to sell world-wide if you wish.

Website design

It is important that your website is professionally designed by someone who knows what they are doing. If your business is computers, your customers may well expect you to be able to design and maintain your own website, but most people starting in business will need the expertise of a professional. Most Business Links and colleges run courses on website design, which is helpful if you are setting up a website for a local club or society, perhaps. Professional website designers will probably advertise in directories, or on-line or through networking. Personal recommendation is often the best.

Your designer will need to know your purpose in having a website. Is it to sell on-line, to give information and contact details about your product or service, or to demonstrate, through animation, what you can do for your clients? For example, a garden landscape designer may wish to conduct you round a garden he or she has designed.

Websites usually start with a Home Page, giving a broad view of your business, and leading your customers into the other pages. It is important that the site is well designed so that potential customers who enter your website can find what they want quickly; if they struggle, they will probably give up. If you are selling on-line you will need a good customer ordering system.

Insight

The most time-consuming part of setting up a website is taking and incorporating photographs, particularly if you are selling small items on-line. Allow as least twice as much time as you think you need.

To start
You will need:

▶ *A modem, linking you to the internet. These are integral to most modern systems*
▶ *An ISP (Internet Service Provider), such as BT, AOL, tiscali, etc.*
▶ *A domain name – the name a website visitor keys in to enter your website. This should be as short and simple as possible, incorporating your business name. The domain name for our business, Chester House Productions, is www.chesterhouse.net. Your website designer will advise you on all these things.*

Broadband or not
Broadband is a package which allows you to upload and download files and graphics far more quickly than the original 'standard' method of transmitting information. If you are likely to transmit or

receive long documents, complicated graphics and/or photographs, broadband is highly desirable. For animation it is essential. You pay for the level of service you need. Again your website designer or your Business Link will advise you.

Website maintenance

Once your site is designed and up and running, you must make arrangements to maintain it, keeping it up-to-date, making sure your ordering and payment systems for your products (if you are selling on-line) is working efficiently and providing you with the statistics you need to monitor your site's efficiency. For simple systems, or if you are computer literate, you could do this yourself, but most businesses rely on their website designer to provide this service. They cannot give you good service, of course, unless you feed them the appropriate information daily, weekly, monthly or as and when, according to your business. There is nothing more off-putting to a potential customer than a website which is out-of-date or says 'Data not available'.

Security

You hear horror stories of viruses, worms and unwanted spam; all these things can happen to you. You should consider an ISP which provides spam filters, parental control (if necessary), a firewall, virus protection, spywear protection, anti-virus software, etc.

Costs

You will need to pay for:

- ▶ *a phone line (for most applications). Broadband allows you to use the same line for internet transmissions and phone calls simultaneously*
- ▶ *the services of your ISP, probably monthly*
- ▶ *your domain name, probably annually*
- ▶ *your website design*
- ▶ *your website maintenance.*

As you can see, the cost of a good website can be considerable and must be taken into account when forming and using your business plan and the cost of your overheads. It is probably wise not to embark on a website too early in your business life, unless you intend to sell exclusively on-line. Get your business off the ground first, particularly if you are manufacturing products, so that you are confident you have plenty of stock to sell. Service providers can afford to start a little earlier.

Marketing your own consultancy

If you are selling a product, you have something tangible to show and demonstrate to prospective customers. If you are running a consultancy, the situation is somewhat different. In effect what you are selling is your time and your expertise. This means that the quality of any materials you produce, not only stationery and advertising, but the actual working documents, must be of the highest standard, both in content and presentation – these are, in fact, your product. Personal presentation must also reflect the standards of your consultancy.

Public Relations (PR) is an effective marketing technique; a means of keeping your consultancy in front of potential clients. Consider sending little snippets of information, or human interest anecdotes relating to you and your consultancy to your specialist publications, association newsletter, or even your local press. Perhaps submitting them on your business paper under the heading PRESS RELEASE will encourage the respective editors to include them in the news sections. This could be a useful and cost-effective way of promoting your consultancy.

Mailshots can be a very effective tool for marketing your consultancy. Study the detailed information about mailshots on pages 59–62, and work out how you can incorporate this method into your marketing plans.

For more general marketing activity, do not be too rigid when targeting your material, particularly where you are offering services relating to universal subjects or interchangeable skills which could potentially cover several categories of business.

A useful tip: if your marketing activity is even more successful than you anticipated, have a contingency plan for excess work – you do not wish to be in the embarrassing situation of having to turn work away. Through your contacts with like-minded people, compile a list of those your consultancy could subcontract to; this way you can be prepared for overlapping jobs. Your contacts would no doubt be happy to reciprocate!

Image

Whichever marketing methods are used, a certain image of the business will be conveyed. An overriding aim should be to make sure that anybody's first contact with the business receives the right impression. This means that attention to detail is important. For example:

YOUR NAME AND LOGO

The name and logo you choose for your company say a lot about who you are and the product or service you are offering. Your name should project your company image, not contradict it.

Try to indicate in your name the nature of your business: 'Kay's Nursery', for example, does not tell customers whether you are dealing with plants or babies. 'Kay's Garden Centre' or 'Kay's Day Nursery' does.

Your logo should also convey clearly what your business is about. You do not necessarily need a drawing – a distinctive typeface and the colour of your stationery will often convey as much as is necessary.

Take care that your name and logo are unique to you and that you are not imitating another company's name or logo.

You can protect your own trade mark, but take advice from
The Patent Office – www.patent.gov.uk – or The Federation of
Small Businesses – www.fsb.co.uk – or your solicitor.

PREMISES

Whether you work from home or 'proper' business premises, an
important and lasting impression of your business will be gained by
people entering your office space for the first time.

VEHICLES

Whether you use your own vehicle, which has a certain anonymity
when driving along the road, or a commercial vehicle which
has your company name painted on the side, an image is being
conveyed to those who see it. If you arrive at a potential client's
premises in a smart, clean vehicle, you are bound to create a more
favourable image than if you arrive in a rusty old banger.

Insight

If you know you are going to have to park inconveniently to
offload goods, and your vehicle does not have any company
name or logo on it, make a readable card you can put on
your dashboard to identify your company. If someone
urgently needs you to move, they will have some clue about
where to find you.

You might think that a prospective customer could be put off by
the sight of an expensive car, believing that if the business can
afford to run such an exotic vehicle its fees or prices must be high.
It is however more likely to evoke the subconscious feeling that this
must be a successful enterprise. A personalized number plate can
look prestigious – and disguise the age of your vehicle.

TELEPHONE

Does your business have a policy about answering the telephone?
If you are the business, who answers the telephone in your absence?

Perhaps you have an answering machine or voicemail: have you rung it up to see what your message sounds like – is it caller-friendly? Does it go on for too long?

A simple policy for your business to adopt could be to ensure that the caller realizes quickly that the correct connection has been made, and that somebody is there willing and able to help – this is an excellent image-maker.

Your customers will expect you to have a mobile phone. Check the different tariffs and networks carefully to make sure you have the right facilities and tariff for your particular business. For example, if you make and receive a lot of calls, a higher rental and many free calls may be desirable. If you do not make many calls, a Pay As You Go system might suffice. You can transfer your mobile number between systems and networks, which takes a little perseverance, but it does mean your company stationery remains up to date.

LETTER AND EMAIL DESIGN

Consider the design of your stationery, not only what information needs to be on it, but how it is laid out. Have a look around at the display boards in the instant-print shops and you will see plenty of examples of what other businesses do. Some you will like, some you will not.

Try to decide what it is about those you like, and see how you could design yours to give an equally favourable impression to those who will be receiving it. While you are about it, think about having the letterheads, compliments slips and business cards all done together so that you have a continuity of design and presentation – again this is good for the image (see Chapter 10).

Having got a decent letterhead, do not spoil the effect by using it for unsightly letters. The layout of letters, faxes, emails, price lists or other tabulated material, can say a lot about your business. Set a standard for the presentation of your written business matter, it can have no small influence on the image of your business (see Chapter 10).

Emails can look impersonal and uninteresting, so design your emails to look attractive to the reader. Think about: incorporating your company name and logo; typeface; typesize; the use of colour. Take care not to over-elaborate: too many graphics can make downloading your emails too lengthy so that recipients will not bother to download and read them.

ADVERTISING MATTER

Whatever type of advertising matter you decide to adopt, do consider the general image it conveys of your business. Much of what has been said about presentation above, can be applied equally well to advertising matter.

Insight

Do your marketing when you are busy, not when you're quiet. You're probably quiet because you didn't do your marketing when you were busy.

PERSONNEL

Probably, when it really comes down to it, it is the people within the business who have the greatest effect on its image. A decently designed piece of headed notepaper will look its best whatever is going on around it. People, however, are different and respond to their surroundings. This is why the people involved in the business must realize that their attitude and general demeanour will make or break the image of the business. This means on occasion submerging personal feelings.

We said at the beginning of this chapter that you need to let people know that your business exists. We have seen that this is not only done by the individuals within the business, but that other, inanimate things have a bearing. In the end it is the actual people who create the most lasting image, which must be a favourable one.

CHECKLIST

▶ **Your marketing profile:**
  ▷ *Have you completed your self-question checklist?*

▶ **Marketing methods:**
  Which is the best for your business?
  ▷ *Advertisements*
  ▷ *Mailshots*
  ▷ *Leaflet drops*
  ▷ *Personal contact*
  ▷ *Trade shows and exhibitions*
  ▷ *Your website*

▶ **Image:**
  What image do the following convey?
  ▷ *Your name and logo*
  ▷ *Your premises*
  ▷ *Your vehicles*
  ▷ *Your telephone answering person or machine*
  ▷ *Your letters, faxes and emails*
  ▷ *Your advertising material*
  ▷ *Your people*

6

Selling the product or service

In this chapter:
- *Preparation*
- *The approach*
- *Establishing the customer's needs*
- *Features and benefits*
- *Objections*
- *Closing*
- *Additional sales and services*

This chapter is not about retailing, where people come to you to buy. It is about selling your product or service to potential customers on their territory, or possibly on neutral territory, such as a hotel coffee lounge.

Preparation

Each potential customer is different, and will want to buy your product or service for slightly different reasons.

Find out as much as you can about the company or client – name, history, background, image, sales potential. Study their advertisements, their stationery, their website and anything else which will give you information about them. You will have to fit into their image of themselves. For example, if when speaking to you or writing to you they have automatically called you by your first name, you know they will want the same approach from you. If their stationery is of top quality, and correspondence is well written and presented, it will tell you a lot about the client's or company's image of themselves. It will tell you, for example, that they or their employers invest time and money in creating a high-quality product or service. They will expect you to do the same.

Remember to take with you samples, leaflets, models – anything to enhance your own presentation. Take your business card and your diary, for future appointments.

Remind yourself of how this particular meeting was generated, especially if you have several calls to make, and have the names of the people you are going to meet firmly in your mind.

Set yourself an objective for this particular meeting, which might be one of several. For example, if this is your first meeting, your objective might be to set a date when you can demonstrate your product or meet the real decision maker. If it is a later meeting, your objective might be to clinch the sale. Do not expect to achieve everything in one meeting, particularly if you are after a sizeable contract, but do try to achieve the objective you have set yourself.

The approach

For a first meeting, the way you approach your potential client or customer is very important.

Unless you are meeting on neutral ground, you will be entering your customer's territory. Take note of whoever greets you: build up a friendly relationship with receptionists, secretaries and any other 'support' people. If you are visiting people's houses, remember to greet other members of the household if you meet them. Remember in both cases to say thank you for any refreshments provided. These people are all part of your customer's background and team, and can often be a help to you in the future.

Insight

Be decisive about accepting tea or coffee offers. Know what you want and state it clearly. Indecision at this stage doesn't give a good first impression.

Take note, too, of the environment. Is the place smart, tidy, fashionable, upmarket, disorganized, scruffy or what? Make allowances for working conditions in, say, a factory or warehouse and match your approach to the environment in which you find yourself. A chaotic place of work might mean a chaotic way of doing business. This is not to say that you must lower your standards in any way, but you should try to attune yourself to your customer's ambience.

Once you have greeted your customer with a handshake and called him or her by the appropriate name, you will probably be expected to make the opening remarks. It is useful to be able to refer to a letter you have written, or a leaflet or sample you have sent; have a spare copy handy in case yours has got mislaid by your customer. Do not at this stage try to go through all the good things about your product or service; it is very tempting to reel these off, but you might not be meeting the needs of that particular customer. Before trying to sell your product or service, you must establish what those needs are.

Insight

A truism: you never get a second chance to make a first impression.

Establishing the customer's needs

You want to find out why your customer or client needs your product or service. To do this you must get your customer talking and be very clear in your mind how your product or service is going to meet those needs.

You could ask your customers to fill you in on what the requirements actually are. For example, if you are trying to land a contract to supply executive lunches in the boardroom, it would be helpful to know, before you start displaying your wares, whether this is a new idea for this company or whether they are dissatisfied with their present caterers, what sort of catering they had in mind and whether this is likely to be a one-off job or a longer contract. This information will then guide you into the sort of service you can offer and the cost, before getting down to details of menu, time, number, and so on.

To develop the conversation along informative lines, you will need to ask questions. Broadly speaking there are two sorts of question – open and closed.

OPEN QUESTIONS

These are questions which begin with words like 'who', 'what', 'when', 'where', 'why' and 'how'. They cannot be answered by a simple 'yes' or 'no', and force the person answering to give you at least some information. For example, 'How have you organized these lunches in the past?' might prompt the person to answer 'We haven't, this is a new idea', or 'Well, we've dropped them recently, because we weren't too happy with them.' You have gained a lot more information than if you had asked, 'Is this a new idea for you?' (a closed question), to which the reply could be either 'Yes' or 'No'.

Open questions are very useful for getting customers to open up and explain fully what their needs are.

CLOSED QUESTIONS

As you have seen, these are questions which can invite a 'yes' or 'no' answer, and are less useful for drawing information out of people.

They can be useful if you want the customer to come to a decision, or make a choice. 'Would you prefer hot or cold?' will prompt either a definite choice or at least lead your customer down one road or the other. 'Shall I be here at 11.00 or 11.30?' stands more chance of getting a definite answer than 'What time would you like me here?'

Continue questioning and clarifying until you are clear about what your customer or client actually wants. If it is obvious to you that what you have to offer does not in any way meet the requirements, it is better to say so than waste your time or your customer's by trying to sell something totally unsuitable or something that you cannot deliver. Do not be put off by objections (which are dealt with later in this chapter), nor by the customer's inability to see that your product or service would be of some benefit. Stop selling at this point only if you are quite sure your product or service is unacceptable.

Insight

Leading questions contain the answer in the question, such as 'So you'll want soft drinks as well, won't you?' This leads the customer to say 'Yes'. Be careful with these, they can be manipulative.

Features and benefits

People buy for different reasons. At this point you have discovered what your client's or customer's real needs are. Now is the time to do two things: describe the features of your product or service, and sell the benefits.

The features are facts, the benefits are the good reasons why your customer should want your product or service – it is benefits which you must sell.

> ## Insight
> Next time someone is selling something to you, notice whether they are selling you the features or the benefits. For example, if you are buying a jacket, does the salesperson emphasize it is cut in a certain style (a feature) or that that style is fashionable (a benefit)? Analysing what other people do helps with your own selling skills.

To return to the executive luncheon service, listed below are some probable features and facts about the service and the allied benefits.

Executive Luncheon Service

Features	Benefits
All food prepared elsewhere and brought in	Client would save staff time buying in and preparing food
Waiter/waitress service	Prestige of expert attention to client's own customers
Wide choice of menu	Variety of tastes and dietary requirements catered for
All products bought fresh (not frozen, etc.)	Excellent quality of food
Large selection of wines	Flexible to meet cost requirements
All table preparation and cleaning done	No staff time taken

If your questioning revealed that these lunches had previously been done in-house, then you would emphasize the benefit of saving staff time. If it were a new idea for the company, you would mention the prestige attached to outside caterers.

You would not approach a potential customer or client without a full knowledge of your product or service, and what you can deliver; the skill is to match your product to the client's requirements by selling the benefits.

It is helpful to make a list of the features and likely benefits of your product or service so that you can call them quickly to mind in a selling situation.

Objections

A customer or client often has genuine objections to your product or service. Do not look upon this as an insurmountable obstacle, but as an opportunity to guide the client in the right direction by overcoming those objections.

MISUNDERSTANDINGS

Objections sometimes arise through misunderstandings or misinterpretations in both directions. If a customer says something like 'Yes, but I'm not too sure ...' try to find out where the uncertainty lies by asking questions and probing into the area of doubt. It might be that the customer has misheard or mis-read something, or that you have not explained it clearly. It might be that you have not understood what the client meant. Keep clarifying until you do, and then clear up the misunderstanding.

For example, if the 'Executive Luncheon' client said, 'I'm not too sure about salmon mousse as a starter', it might be that you had given the impression that salmon mousse was the only starter available or that you had not understood that the client does not like fish. In either event by asking, 'What would you prefer as a starter?' you will probably elicit enough information to clear up the point.

Misunderstandings?   clarify and explain

SCEPTICISM

Sometimes customers or clients are doubtful about the capacity of your product or service to meet their needs. If they say something like 'Yes, but I can't see how ...' you must reassure them by proving that your product or service will meet their needs.

This is the time to quote definite facts or demonstrate the product. You can show relevant tables of figures, make good estimates of time and/or money saved or literally demonstrate the product there and then.

If the 'Executive Luncheon' client said, 'I don't see how you can get the boardroom clear in a quarter of an hour', you could quote other examples (named clients) of where you had done just that, or you could take the client quickly through the timings, emphasizing the fact that everything is brought in easily packed trays.

....
        Scepticism?   *give proof*
....

PRICE

One of the most common objections is the cost. You must be very sure in your own mind how low you can go in accepting a lower cost, and be flexible down to that point. You can emphasize the fact that VAT is recoverable (if it is); you should also re-state the agreed benefits to the customer.

You might be able to go lower on one point (perhaps reduce the delivery charge) while sticking on another. Sometimes it is better to quote for the whole package, while emphasizing what the package contains. At others it is useful to 'unbundle' the package (cost each element separately) so the client can buy at least some of it.

Try not to let the customer buy only the least profitable parts of the package. For example, the 'Executive Luncheon' firm would be unwise to let the client provide the wine, because that is probably the most profitable part of the business. However, if such a deal were to lead to a long and good contract, the firm might decide to let it go this time and re-negotiate another time.

> *Price?* remind the customer of the agreed benefits
> be prepared to negotiate, but know your limits

Closing

The customer will eventually give an indication that he or she is ready to bring the meeting to a close. The signs might be verbal: 'Well, if you would like to let me have a copy of those figures for Monday morning ...' or 'Yes, I like what you're offering, but I need to consult my colleagues'. The signs might be non-verbal – nodding, leaning forward, hands on thighs, standing up. A good book on body language and how it can help a salesperson is *Body Language* by Allan Pease, published by Sheldon Press or *Teach Yourself Body Language* by Geoff Ribbens and Greg Whitear and obtainable from most good bookshops.

When you receive these closing signals, STOP SELLING. More than one sale has been lost by the salesperson over-emphasizing agreed benefits or, worse still, introducing benefits not mentioned before, which only confuse the customer. It is not easy to stop yourself from telling the customer all the benefits of your product or service, but once the closing signals have been given, you must stop selling.

Summarize what has been agreed between you. If a new meeting is to be arranged, try to arrange it then and there – get your diary out and suggest dates and times. If a senior executive asks you to make an appointment with his or her secretary, make it with the secretary and do not try to force the executive to make the appointment. If you are to provide further information, establish exactly when and where it is to be delivered. If your customer is to let you have further information, try to get a definite commitment on what it is and the anticipated timing. If the person to whom you are speaking is not the decision maker, try to make sure that your product or service gets presented to the decision maker. Try to get a name, and offer to write or meet to demonstrate the product – anything to take the matter a step further.

If you are able to clinch the sale at that meeting, make sure that all costs, delivery dates and so on are agreed, and get a signature if possible. Immediately after the meeting write and confirm the terms of the agreement, set out very clearly what you are supplying, what the costs are and what the terms of payment are (see Chapter 7). If you think it more than likely that this meeting will be the one where you finally make the sale, you can have all this paperwork ready with you, but do not produce it too early in the proceedings.

Insight
Once you receive the buying signals STOP SELLING.

At the close of the meeting, each party should be clear about what is to happen next on both sides. This applies to a service rendered in someone's home just as much as it does to a product sold to a large company. Shake hands to conclude the meeting.

As you leave, remember to say goodbye to support staff or other members of the household, and thank them for anything they have done for you.

Finally, when you get back to your own place of work, do everything that you have promised to do, and do it promptly.

Additional sales and services

Sometimes there is an opportunity to offer additional sales or services; the skill here lies in seizing the opportunity but not being too pushy about it.

You might be able, in the course of selling a package, to suggest a small extra which would enhance the end product or service and make extra sales for you. The 'Executive Luncheon' firm might be able to introduce their printed menu service; an office services bureau might suggest website management.

If you cannot introduce these additional sales and services during the selling process, you might be able to leave a leaflet or some other advertising material as you conclude your business. Never travel without your publicity material, and leave it behind if possible, without forcing it on your customers or clients.

CHECKLIST

▶ **Preparation:**
  ▷ *What do you know about your potential client or customer?*
  ▷ *Who are you going to meet?*
  ▷ *Have you got everything you need, including publicity material for additional sales and services?*
  ▷ *What are your objectives for this meeting?*

▶ **Approach:**
  ▷ *Build relationships with 'support' people.*
  ▷ *Note the environment.*
  ▷ *Shake hands and use the appropriate name.*
  ▷ *Refer to something already done or sent.*

▶ **Establish needs:**
  ▷ *Ask questions: open questions help to clarify; closed questions help choices and decisions.*
  ▷ *Get the customer talking.*

▶ **Features and benefits:**
  ▷ *Make a list of the features and benefits of your product or service.*
  ▷ *Describe the features/facts – demonstrate if appropriate.*
  ▷ *Sell the benefits.*

▶ **Objections:**
  ▷ *Misunderstanding – clarify and explain.*
  ▷ *Scepticism – give proof.*
  ▷ *Price – remind the customer of the agreed benefits; be prepared to negotiate, but know your limits.*

▶ **Closing:**
  ▷ *Stop selling.*
  ▷ *Summarize what has been agreed.*
  ▷ *Agree action plan.*

▶ **Additional sales and services:**
   ▷ *Introduce during the selling process if possible.*
   ▷ *Leave publicity material at the conclusion of the meeting, but do not force it.*

▶ *DID YOU ACHIEVE YOUR OBJECTIVE?*

7

Doing the books

In this chapter:
- *Receipts and payments*
- *Petty cash*
- *VAT*
- *Banking*
- *Necessary or useful records*
- *Manual or computer*
- *Year end*

Next to stocktaking, many business people consider doing the books a necessary chore. The key to successful, and not excessively time-consuming, book-keeping is to have a workable system, to keep to it, and so keep on top of the workload.

This chapter describes doing the books manually, followed by advice on book-keeping on your desktop or laptop.

Insight

For businesses selling products, a computerized system is probably better (see pages 103–5). For consultancies and small businesses with few invoices, a manual system is easy to maintain and takes a couple of hours on a Saturday morning.

Receipts and payments

Broadly speaking, the books of a business are divided into two sections, one to record moneys coming in and the other to record moneys going out. An average small business does not need to have a complicated system of book-keeping, but it does need to show clearly the incomings and outgoings of the business, and dates when the transactions took place.

A very simple system could look like this:

Receipts				Payments			
Date	Description	£	p	Date	Description	£	p

However, it would not be very practical, because you will want to analyse receipts and payments (particularly payments) under different headings at the time of recording the details in the books: this can be done with very little effort or trouble. It is important to analyse your purchases, or payments, to keep track at regular intervals, and particularly year on year, of your outgoings. Without this analysis, you would not know, for example, how much your fuel bills had increased.

A basic loose-leaf accounts system has advantages for a new business. It is worth making a visit to a shop which specializes in this type of business stationery and studying the options. There are some well-known brand names in this area. Decide what you want your account sheets to do, and find the most appropriate ones for the job.

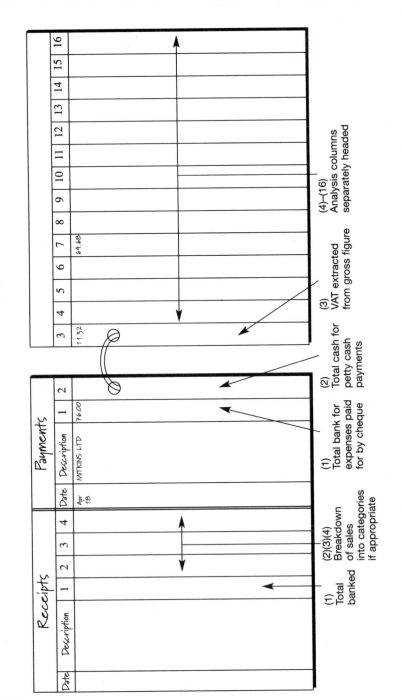

Receipts

Date	Description	1	2	3	4

(1) Total banked

(2)(3)(4) Breakdown of sales into categories if appropriate

Payments

Date	Description	1	2
Apr 18	MITKINS LTD	76.00	

(1) Total bank for expenses paid for by cheque

(2) Total cash for petty cash payments

3	4	5	6	7	8	9	10	11	12	13	14	15	16
11.52				64.68									

(3) VAT extracted from gross figure

(4)–(16) Analysis columns separately headed

90

For the main record keeping, a standard 11¾ ins × 14 ins (297 × 356 mm) sheet with four columns for receipts and 16 columns for payments would probably be suitable.

It is useful to insert a folio number, such as page number and line number (01/01 for the first line of the first page). If these numbers are entered onto invoices/receipts it makes for an easier audit trail.

A basic loose leaf account layout could look something like the example opposite.

Insight

When paying bills or invoices, note on the invoice or bill the number and date of the cheque paid out, and ring round it in red. Your auditor will be able to see it quickly and check it with the bank statement – and so will you.

A typical payment entry made by cheque would show, apart from the date and who was being paid, the gross amount in the Total Bank column (Column 1), the amount of VAT (Column 3), with the net amount in the appropriate analysis column (Columns 4–16). If there was no VAT involved, the amount in the analysis column would be the same as that in the Total Bank column.

It is sometimes possible that items in one transaction apply to more than one analysis column. In this case, enter the amounts in the appropriate columns, and check to see that everything adds across to the figure in the Total Bank column (Column 1).

A suitable breakdown of payments could be as follows, with each heading having its own column across the page:

Materials	Entertainment
Light/heat	Subsistence/hotel
Petrol/travel	Capital equipment
Vehicle expenses	Advertising
Telephone and postage	Rent/rates
Printing and stationery	Insurances

It would also be useful to segregate out payments like:

Bank charges and interest
Money withdrawn from the bank for Petty Cash replenishment
DWP deductions
Tax and VAT payments to HM Revenue & Customs

Another necessary column would show any drawings or directors' fees made from the business account for personal use.

One indispensable column for those payments which for one reason or another will not fit into any other column is the one headed Sundries, and would probably be the final one on the sheet.

If you find you need more headings than will comfortably fit into Columns 4 to 16 on one sheet, use a second analysis sheet. Ask your accountant to advise you on the headings most appropriate to your business.

Cross-check all figures each time a sheet is completed. It is worth taking time to do this so that any errors in calculation can be highlighted quickly, and you can move onto the new sheet confident that all is accurate.

As well as totalling each sheet as it is completed, the sheets should be ruled off at suitable intervals – weekly, monthly, quarterly – depending on what is most appropriate for your business.

As supplementary sheets for recording Sales or Petty Cash, a standard 11¾ ins × 8¼ ins (297 × 210 mm) sheet with four or five columns would enable you to record the facts needed.

For example, for Invoiced Sales:

Invoiced Sales			(1)	(2)	(3)	(4)
Date	Description	INV.	Gross	VAT	Net	Payment received
MAR 21	DEGEMA LTD	3821	702.53	104.63	597.90	MAY 8

Having a Payment Received column (Column 4) enables you to
see at a glance how many outstanding invoices there are at any
one time.

If your business is involved in Cash Sales, you would probably
find it easier and more convenient to keep a separate record sheet
for those.

A Petty Cash Record could be as straightforward at this:

Petty Cash Record			(1)	(2)	(3)	(4)
Date	Description	Week no.	IN	OUT	Balance	
	Opening balance		25.00	–	25.00	
w/e MAR 6	Expenses	①		6.10	18.90	
w/e MAR 13	Expenses	②		12.19	6.71	
MAR 21	Replenishment		50.00		56.71	

It is, as you can see, a control or summary sheet. It is a very useful way of keeping an eye on the balance, to know when the petty cash float needs replenishing.

We will look at the detail behind these expense figures under the *Petty cash* section of this chapter, below.

If it suits the pattern of your business, for both these sheets you could rule them off each month. Apart from anything else, it means if the figures do not balance, there is only one month's work to check!

Petty cash

Petty cash is a sum of money used for small, everyday expense items. These day-to-day business expenses need to be properly recorded.

It is a good practical idea to have a small (160 x 100 mm)
Cash Book, which it is easy to carry about, in which to record
expenses as they happen. It is a very useful habit to get into.
For example, when you buy the train ticket, or the supply of
postage stamps, write the amount in your Petty Cash Book
straight away.

At the end of, say, each week, the details of the expenses in
your Petty Cash Book are recorded on the main account sheet,
with the total figure of each expenditure being written in the
Total Cash column (Column 2) with any VAT in Column 3
and the net figures in the appropriate analysis column
(Columns 4–16).

The total amount of the weekly expenditure is recorded on the
Petty Cash Record sheet. This is best done when the money is
actually paid out: it also provides a good opportunity to check the
balance in the petty cash tin.

When the money has been reclaimed, the Petty Cash Book should
be marked accordingly. Simply writing 'Reimbursed' across the
entries in red ink could be sufficient.

Try to maintain a system to ensure that each expense claim
is accompanied by a receipt. This is not possible in all cases,
of course; parking meters will not issue a receipt (even though
Traffic Wardens could provide another type of document in
certain circumstances!) but a Pay and Display and multi-storey
car park will provide a receipt. You can get a receipt for train
tickets and the Post Office clerk will give you a receipt for
your stamps if asked: complications can arise in a restaurant

if a group of you wish to have separate bills for your own account records – try mentioning this fact when ordering your meal.

If something is bought in a retail shop as a petty cash expense, it is important that the receipt shows the VAT number of that business. Many, though not all, till receipts show the VAT number of the business issuing it. It is always worth checking, and if there is no number, ask for a VAT receipt.

Insight

When deciding whether a purchase is a business expense or not, ask yourself, 'Am I buying this only for business purposes?' If the answer is 'Yes', it is a business expense.

VAT

Value Added Tax (VAT) is the tax on goods and services as supplied. It is administered on behalf of the government by HM Revenue & Customs (see Chapter 9). We are concerned here about recording VAT in the books of the business. Even if you are not registered for VAT yourself, it could still be worthwhile isolating the VAT from your payments, because it may be possible to claim some of it in retrospect when you register; ask your accountant's advice on this. In any case it is all good practice, and a useful habit to get into.

You, as a business, can only be charged VAT by another organization if that business is itself VAT registered. A VAT registered company must show its nine digit VAT registration number (set out like this: 987 6543 21) on its stationery, particularly its invoices and receipts.

The point is that a VAT registered company can claim back the VAT it has paid on legitimate business expenses. We will cover the method of doing this later in this section.

As far as the books are concerned, the principle of recording an expense involving VAT so as to isolate the VAT figure would be like this:

Date	Description	Gross	VAT	Net
AUG 23	ENVELOPES	2.50	0.37	2.13

On an accounts sheet with analysis columns, the £2.13 would be written in the Stationery column.

When making these entries it is useful to check the maths by cross-casting the figures across the line to ensure that the net figure plus the VAT equals the gross amount. This can save a lot of time – and heartache – when you get to the bottom of the account sheet and have to reconcile all the figures.

It is probably worthwhile at this stage to look at the mechanics of extracting the VAT from a VAT-inclusive price, where the VAT amount is not shown as a separate figure (although an increasing number of till receipts do this).

We will use our envelopes as an example. Basing the above calculation on 17½% VAT, the figures are:

VAT-inclusive price	2.50
17½% VAT	0.37
VAT-exclusive price	£2.13

The answer is easy to see, but how is it arrived at? The solution is not as easy as taking 17½% away from the VAT-inclusive price, because 17½% of £2.50 is more than 17½% of £2.13 (which is the figure we want).

If you do this on a calculator: 2.50 × 17.5% %️ key you will see that the answer is 0.437 and not 0.372 as it should be.

What you have to do is a calculation which is directly related to the VAT rate, and which will change whenever the VAT rate changes. For 17½% the calculation is:

$$\text{VAT-inclusive price} \times 7 \div 47$$

Apply this to our example:

$$2.50 \times 7 = 17.50 \div 47 = 0.372$$

Therefore 2.50 minus 0.37 equals 2.13.

The fraction for 17½% VAT is $\frac{7}{47}$, but remember to find out what the new fraction is if the VAT rate changes.

Translate the above vulgar fraction into decimal form as follows:

$$7 \div 47 \boxed{\%} \text{ key} = 14.893617$$

This will enable you to calculate the amount of VAT in one calculation, i.e.

$$2.50 \times 14.893617 \boxed{\%} \text{ key} = 0.372 = 37p$$

It is important to be able to do this calculation because, although some accounts may be small, if they are added together with the claims for other purchases or expenses (for instance, petrol and parking) they can soon add up to a significant amount.

Insight

Never use your VAT money collected to pay for other things – e.g. wages. HM Revenue & Customs are very good at chasing up VAT payments. Using your VAT money for other purposes is a sure way to failure.

VAT Returns are made quarterly to HM Revenue & Customs. On your VAT Return form you fill in the value of the supplies you have made and received during the tax period, and pay the total tax you owe to HM Revenue & Customs, or claim a repayment if tax is owed to you (which can happen if your expenses have been greater than your receipts).

The VAT Return, and any payment due must reach HM Revenue & Customs by the due date shown on the Return: penalties could be incurred for late payment, particularly if this is consistently happening.

The following extracts from notes supplied by HM Revenue & Customs may provide you with some helpful general background information about VAT.

It is the person, not the business, who is registered for VAT. Each registration covers all the business activities of the registered person.
The person to be registered can be a sole proprietor, a partnership (including husband and wife partnerships), a limited partnership, a limited company, a club or association, or a charity.
If you are a taxable person, you must account for VAT whenever you make a taxable supply. The supply is your output and the VAT is your output tax.
If your customer is registered for VAT and the supply is for the purposes of business, the supply is his input and the tax you charge him is his input tax. In the same way, VAT charged to you on your business purchases is your input tax.

There are many helpful leaflets describing the various aspects of VAT published by HM Revenue & Customs. It is worthwhile paying a visit to your local VAT office – addresses are in the phone book under 'Customs and Excise'.

All your dealings should be with your local VAT office; you only deal with the Head Office at Southend when you send them back your Quarterly Return.

Banking

Insight

Some very small businesses use their personal bank account for their business banking, but it is tiresome to have to annotate each entry into 'business' or 'personal'.

A new business needs to have its own bank account, and arrangements should be made to open at least a current account. There are a few basic things to be considered and arranged:

You will not receive a cheque guarantee card with a business account – although you can have a cashpoint card.

You will need to provide a sum of money to deposit into the account to make it active (this would be recorded on the account sheets as 'capital introduced').

If there is to be more than one signatory, arrangements should be made with the bank about whether all should sign or whether any one of those designated is sufficient. In any case sample signatures from all signatories will need to be provided.

You will receive a bank statement each month. You may have to ask for this because banks will sometimes only send statements quarterly, particularly for private accounts. This is too long a period for a business account.

Consider whether you need to have an overdraft facility attached to this account. Find out what the arrangement fee will be, and how long the arrangement is to last before it is reviewed; negotiate for as long a period as possible.

The name of the bank account needs to be decided. Will it be in the name of the business only, or perhaps in the name of the sole trader? Will it have the name of the person and the business name, for instance Arthur Cosford T/A Arco Services?

A paying in book will be necessary for depositing cheques and moneys received by the business.

A business bank account is bound to attract bank charges, even if it is only after an interest-free period, which some banks advertise for new business accounts. You will recall we suggested having a column to record these on the account analysis sheets. You may be paying interest charges from the start.

Consider whether you need to open a deposit account, where moneys not immediately needed could be placed to earn some interest. This, or any other suitable form of interest-earning account, could be useful for putting aside moneys in anticipation of the next VAT Return. Remember, if you charge VAT on your goods or supplies, a proportion of the money you receive ($17\frac{1}{2}\%$ at present) will be required by HM Revenue & Customs. Beware of thinking you are better off than you really are and unwittingly spending your VAT money.

BANK STATEMENTS

When you receive a bank statement for your business account, you need to check the details against the entries on your account sheets. This need not be a complicated exercise; simply tick (in red so that it will show up easily) the statement and the equivalent entry in your account sheets. Keep each statement carefully with your records, your accountant will need them when auditing your books.

You may well find items on the bank statement which you have not recorded on your account sheets. The bank charges and/or interest will probably be one. In this case, write in the amount on the account sheet and tick both this entry and the statement. It can be useful to include in the entry on the account sheets the statement number where the charges appeared; this could well help your accountant reconcile the figures at some future date.

This is quite a useful general principle to follow when doing the books: ask yourself when writing in a transaction, 'Will this make sense to somebody looking at it sometime in the future?' (your accountant, the VAT officer, HM Revenue & Customs). If there is any doubt at all, make a little note as a reminder – it could save you a grilling from any of the above-mentioned parties, with you racking your brains trying to remember the details or circumstances.

Other items on a business bank statement which have not been recorded on your account sheets could be Direct Debit deduction – for instance DWP Insurance. These can vary in amount, depending on the number of weeks in the month covered by the statement. As before, write the details onto your account sheets – allocate a separate column to record these outgoings – tick them, and note the statement number on the account sheet for future reference.

Most banks now offer a free, secure on-line banking service. Once the on-line registration is completed, you should be able to view your bank balances and transactions, manage your standing orders and direct debits, pay bills, transfer money between your accounts and print statements. This could be more convenient than visiting the High Street, as you can access the sites 24 hours a day.

SECURITY

Your business activities will no doubt involve you in making visits to the bank from time to time. If you need to make regular visits, particularly for the purpose of depositing or withdrawing cash, consider the security implications, not only for the money but for yourself or your personnel.

Simple devices like varying the time and the route, and perhaps the people, could help to avoid any unpleasantness en route.

Necessary or useful records

Records and various statistics are kept and maintained by a business. These will obviously vary according to the type of business, and the use which can be made of the data they contain.

We have tried to prepare a checklist of those records it is necessary – a legal requirement – to keep, and those which it could be useful to have. Use it as a basis for compiling one which would be relevant for your business.

Necessary

Accounting sheets and ancillary documents

Bank statements

Receipts for payments made

Sales invoices

VAT records, including VAT Returns

Computer audit trails

Useful

Breakdown of sales – by time or product or both

Comparison figures – between different parts of the business or last week/last year

Insight

At the end of each month, quarter or year, make a graph of your sales. It will easily reveal peaks and troughs and whether your year-on-year sales are increasing or declining. You can also make charts or graphs of your most profitable lines and your best type of customer. We in Chester House Productions keep records of all our venues, productions and audience numbers, so we can tell which of our productions are the most popular and our total and average audiences for each.

Manual or computer

What we have described in this chapter is a basic manual system for doing the books, which could be the best way to start.

As your business progresses and expands, you may well consider developing its systems to something more mechanical – take your accountant's advice before you embark on anything definite.

The sort of thing which might be suitable to consider is an accounts package on a desktop or laptop. Systems vary in sophistication.

You can get systems in which for your *sales*, you key in the amount of goods supplied and details about price, settlement terms, VAT rates and so on and the system will do all the calculations for you, print out an invoice and add the required amount to your VAT Return at the end of the quarter.

For *purchases*, again you key in the details of the purchase and how payment is to be made; the system will produce a list of cheques to be made out (sometimes the cheques themselves). The amount of VAT you can claim will be automatically added to your VAT Return. The total of your net sales and purchases is then added as the actual figures on your Cash Flow Forecast (see Chapter 2) so that you can see at a glance how well your business is doing.

Do not rush into buying computer software for your book-keeping, particularly if you are fairly new to computers. You need to buy the software which is right for your business. You might decide in the end to computerize only part of it.

There are many different software packages on the market today that deal with basic accounts information and are easy to use. The most common and easily available are Sage and Quickbooks (see *Teach Yourself Sage Line 50* by MacBride). The advantage of using one of these packages is that they have good telephone help lines and most accountants are familiar with them.

Make sure that you keep computerized records carefully. Make back-up disks in case your current disks get corrupted. Your accountant will need your summary printouts (which can usually be generated automatically by the system) for the audit trail. HM Revenue & Customs might require these as well.

If you are running a business with many customer accounts requiring lots of invoices each month, a computerized book-keeping system could save you a lot of time. If you are running say, a consultancy with far fewer invoices and payments, the amount of time saved is minimal.

The other type of package which you might find very useful is a wages package. Once set up, this can, with a minimal amount of keying in, generate pay slips and cheques, so that you know your employees receive all the information and money to which they are entitled (see Chapter 11).

You might consider employing a professional book-keeper to do your books, make your VAT returns and run your wages system. These professionals often run small businesses themselves, and are usually trained in using the latest computerized package.

Year end

At the end of your company's financial year, you will have to submit all your books and accounts to your accountant to audit and present to HM Revenue & Customs. You will not be able to do this until the final bank statement for the year has arrived and been included in your accounts for that year.

If yours is a limited company, remember that the accounts must be submitted to Companies House not later than ten months after the end of the financial year, so it helps your accountant if you are prompt in completing and delivering the year's books or computer printouts.

Insight

There is a system called 'Small Business Exemption' which means *very* small businesses don't have to submit their accounts to Companies House. Your accountant can advise you.

CHECKLIST

▶ *You need to record all transactions. Have you got adequate records, on paper or computer, of the following:*
  ▷ *Sales – goods and services you sell*
  ▷ *Purchases – goods and services you buy*
  ▷ *Banking transactions*
  ▷ *Petty Cash*
  ▷ *VAT Returns?*

▶ *How frequently do you do your books?*

▶ *Does your system let you know how well your business is doing?*

8

....

Personal finances and business expenses

In this chapter:
- *Money for personal use*
- *NI contributions and pensions*
- *Income tax*
- *Allowable business expenses*

In Chapter 2, we considered the financial aspects relating to your product or service. In this chapter we will be looking at various financial implications relating to the individual, especially the way they affect the person who is self-employed. Many of these financial implications have a legal liability.

NB The information as presented in this chapter is liable to change. Please check with your accountant about the most up-to-date position.

Money for personal use

In Chapter 7, we saw that a column is reserved for 'drawings or directors' fees': moneys which are withdrawn from the business for personal use. As a sole trader or a member of a partnership, this could well be done on an as-and-when basis. With a limited company, it is more likely to take the form of a regular amount drawn from the company account in the form of a salary.

NI contributions and pensions

Almost everybody who is self-employed pays towards a basic state pension through making National Insurance (NI) contributions. In Chapter 7, we showed how you should record these on your account sheets if you are paying by Direct Debit. There are numerous methods of payment – ask the DWP for details.

The amount you have to pay depends partly on the amount of your taxable business profit. Most self-employed individuals have to pay Class 2 contributions. Above a certain profit level individuals must pay Class 4 contributions. Some is paid by monthly contributions and some is paid at the same time as your income tax. Ask your accountant for details.

Self-employed people cannot get SERPS (State Earnings Related Pension Scheme), on the basic state pension. If you are self-employed you can get tax relief on payments to a Personal Pension Plan (PPP). This is one of the best forms of investment you can make. Do your pension sums well ahead of retirement: once your pension starts to be paid, you will not be able to take a cash lump sum.

Insight

Listen carefully to the pre-budget statements and the Chancellor's budget each year, particularly about National Insurance, pensions and tax. Don't rely on headlines in the media, read the detail as it emerges, and ask your accountant to keep you up to date. Don't ring your accountant on budget day. He or she will be glued to the radio or television and the financial press the next morning.

Income tax

To be treated as self-employed for tax purposes, you must convince your tax office (preferably through your accountant) that you are genuinely in business on your own account, and not an employee. This will depend, amongst other things, on whether you risk your own money or provide major items of equipment, whether you are told what to do, where, when and how – or decide by yourself.

Each HM Revenue & Customs and DWP local office has someone responsible for saying whether or not you will be treated as self-employed, but check with your accountant before approaching them direct.

If you form a limited company, the tax rules are quite different; you pay corporation tax on the business profits, and you will need the help of your accountant to deal with this.

Sole traders and partnerships are taxed in a similar way, but there are special rules for partnerships.

In a partnership the partners are each responsible for the tax on their own income not related to the partnership. The partnership also gets its own tax return. The profit is then divided between the individual partners in proportion to what each gets under the partnership agreement. Each partner's share is taxed at his or her own rate of tax, taking into account other personal income and allowances.

In April 1997 the new self-assessment of income tax came into full force. Self-employed people have to assess their tax liability on the current year's income, and pay the year's tax in two instalments. Your accountant will advise you on what you should do, and there is a range of leaflets available from HM Revenue & Customs.

You will need to submit your self-assessment income tax returns to HM Revenue & Customs by the end of January each year, which your accountant will do for you. If you return your submission by the end of September, HM Revenue & Customs will calculate your income tax for you. If you return it after 31 January, you will have to pay penalties.

Make a note of when you filed your tax return, so that you can prove, if necessary, that it went in on time. From 2010 you must file your return on-line – see HM Revenue & Customs website: www.hmrc.gov.uk.

It is important to sort out your arrangements for self-assessment, because the Inspector of Taxes can audit anyone's return and books at any time. Be sure to keep records of all your transactions – you could be fined if you do not.

Insight

If your income changes dramatically, for example if you decide to close down part of your business, this could well trigger HM Revenue & Customs' computer to enquire into your business and ask to see your books. This happened to us when we decided to give up training and concentrate on acting – far less lucrative. HM Revenue & Customs only have the right to ask to see your business accounts, not your personal transactions. Make sure they work through your accountant.

Allowable business expenses

You can deduct *allowable* business expenses from your profits. An expense will be allowable only if it is incurred 'wholly and exclusively' for the business. This does not mean that you can claim nothing if, for example, you use your car partly for business and partly for private purposes, or use part of your home for business.

You can normally claim the proportion of these costs that is attributable to business use – you will have to agree the proportion with your tax office (preferably via your accountant).

Car expenses are usually shared out according to mileage.

Insight

Every time we go on a business trip (as opposed to personal outings) we make a note of the mileage. This includes visits to local networking meetings, meetings with solicitors and accountants etc. At the end of the year, we note our total mileage, then the running total of your business mileage can easily be declared as a percentage of the whole. It's a bit tedious, but better than estimating it. If we forget to do this, we estimate the mileage by checking an internet route planner.

If you are self-employed (or have some freelance or sparetime work) and do part of your work at home, you can normally claim, as an allowable expense, the proportion of the cost of running your home attributable to business use. You will have to agree with your tax office – through your accountant – what proportion of telephone, heating bills, etc. you can claim.

If you devote part of your home, a room, say, exclusively to business use, you may be able to claim a proportion of rent and council tax – usually based on the number and size of rooms, BUT exclusive use for business purposes may mean some capital gains tax to pay when you sell – check with your accountant.

Circumstances vary considerably, but the sort of business expenses which might be allowable – or not allowable – could be:

Normally allowed	Not allowed
Basic costs and general running expenses:	
Cost of goods bought for re-sale and raw materials used in business	Initial cost of:
Advertising	▶ machinery
Delivery charges	▶ vehicles
Heating and lighting	▶ equipment
	▶ permanent advertising signs

(Contd)

Normally allowed	Not allowed

Cleaning
Rates and rent of business premises
Telephone and postage
Replacement of small tools and
  special clothing
Stationery
Relevant books and magazines
Accountant's fees
Bank charges on business accounts
Subscriptions to professional and
  trade organizations

Use of home for work:
Proportion of:
  ▶ telephone
  ▶ lighting
  ▶ heating
  ▶ cleaning
  ▶ insurance

Proportion of rent and rates if part
  of home is used exclusively for
  business (but beware of Capital
  Gains Tax)

Normally allowed	Not allowed

Wages and salaries:

- Wages, salaries, redundancy and reasonable leaving payments paid to employees
- Pensions for ex-employees and their dependants

Training costs for employees to acquire or improve skills needed for their current job, and re-training costs for employees who are leaving

Your own wages or salary or that of any partner

Tax and National Insurance:

Employers National Insurance contributions for employees

VAT on allowable business expenses if you are a VAT registered trader

Income Tax
Capital Gains tax
Inheritance tax
Your own National Insurance contributions

Entertaining:

Entertainment of your staff:

- Ex gratia payments not paid in lieu of wages
- A 'modest' expenditure (about £150 per employee to include partners) is allowed for Christmas or other annual entertainment

Any business entertaining

Gifts:

Gifts so long as the gift advertises your business

Food, drink, tobacco gifts or vouchers for goods given to anyone other than employees

(Contd)

Normally allowed	Not allowed

Insurance:

Business insurance premiums e.g.
- employer's liability
- fire and theft
- motor
- employees' Life Cover

Premiums for your own:
- life insurance
- accident insurance
- sickness insurance

Travelling and subsistence:

Cost of travel and accommodation on business trips

Reasonable cost of dinner and breakfast – but not lunch – on overnight trips

Travel between different places of work

Running costs of own car: whole of cost, excluding depreciation if used privately too

Travel between home and business

Cost of buying car or van

Interest payments:

Interest on, and costs of arranging, overdrafts and loans for business purposes

Interest on capital paid or credited to partners

Interest on overdue tax

Hiring:

Reasonable charge for hire of capital goods, including cars

Trade marks, designs and patents:

Fees paid to register trade mark or design, or to obtain a patent

Cost of buying patent

Normally allowed	Not allowed

Legal costs:

Cost of:

- ▶ recovering debts
- ▶ defending business rights
- ▶ preparing service agreements
- ▶ appealing against rates on business premises
- ▶ renewing lease, with landlord's consent, for 50 years or less (but not if premium paid)

Expenses (including stamp duty) for acquiring land, buildings or leases

Fines and other penalties for breaking the law

Costs of fighting a tax case

Repairs:

Normal repairs and maintenance to premises or equipment

Costs of additions, alterations or improvements

Subscriptions/contributions:

Payments which secure benefits for your business and staff

Genuine contribution to approved local Enterprise Agency

Payments to professional bodies which have arrangements with HM Revenue & Customs (in some cases only a proportion of the payment can be claimed)

Payments to:

- ▶ political parties
- ▶ places of worship
- ▶ charities

(Small gifts to local charities may be allowable)

Capital expenditure:

Nothing allowed

Capital expenditure (i.e. what you spend on buying cars, machinery, etc.) is not an allowable expense

Depreciation of equipment (This would be dealt with by your accountant under Capital Allowances)

CHECKLIST

▶ *What arrangements have you made for drawing money out of your company for personal expenditure?*

▶ *What arrangements have you made to pay your NI contributions?*

▶ *Which personal pension plan do you have? If none, start to make arrangements now.*

▶ *Have you agreed with HM Revenue & Customs and the DWP that you are self-employed?*

▶ *Do you claim all allowable business expenses?*

▶ *Do you keep a note of your business mileage?*

▶ *Do you claim any business expenses which are not allowable? If you do, HM Revenue & Customs can say that your books are incorrect, and can ask to see and check everything in great detail.*

HM Revenue & Customs' website (www.hmrc.gov.uk) is an excellent reference source.

9

....

The professionals

In this chapter:
- *How to find the professionals*
- *Accountants*
- *Architects*
- *Banks and building societies*
- *Estate agents*
- *HM Revenue & Customs (VAT)*
- *Insurance brokers*
- *Printers*
- *Office services*
- *Solicitors*

This chapter outlines the specialist services you may need to help you set up your business, to expand it and to keep it going. Some of the things listed here you may be able to do for yourself, but when you need professional help, get the best you can afford.

How to find the professionals

You should be able to find all these professional services listed in *Yellow Pages*, Thomson and other local directories, but how do you know which one to pick?

You often know or have used the services of at least one of these before – a banker or a solicitor perhaps. If they seem to be business-like and helpful, they are a good place to start, and can often recommend other services. For example, a banker can sometimes recommend an accountant, an estate agent can recommend an architect or a printer can recommend some secretarial services.

Your local Business Link can perhaps point you in the right direction, and your public library often has lists available. Read the advertisements in the local and national newspapers to see what banks and building societies are offering, or look under the Classified Advertisements for services such as printers and accountants. You will find the local VAT office in the telephone directory under HM Customs and Excise. Their website address is www.hmrc.gov.uk.

Insight

Government departments are excellent at giving technical help on legal obligations and what you have to do to comply with various regulations. They are not normally there to give in-depth personal advice on your lifestyle. Her Majesty's Inspectors of Taxes just don't do that sort of thing.

Probably the best source of finding the right professional advice is the personal recommendation of someone you know and trust. Very large organizations, such as banks and building societies, do tend to vary, depending on the local manager.

Insight

It's a good idea to deal with professionals who are themselves self-employed small businesses. They will understand your business, and their business relies on giving you first-class advice and service.

Accountants

A good accountant will be one of your best assets. Accountants can render the following main services:

▶ *Book-keeping (see Chapter 7)*
▶ *VAT returns*

- *Annual trading accounts*
- *Tax returns*
- *Help with Cash Flow Forecasts*

Many small businesses do the book-keeping and VAT returns themselves and leave their accountant to do the more complicated jobs of the annual trading accounts and negotiations with HM Revenue & Customs. A qualified accountant is essential for Limited Companies. You might consider employing a professional book-keeper to do the books.

Do not expect an accountant to present your annual accounts to you within about a month of the end of your financial year. They usually take a great deal longer than this, but you should expect them to deal promptly with HM Revenue & Customs matters; if they do not, you might have to pay interest on unpaid tax.

Insight

The professionals do not tell you what to do. They give advice, based on their knowledge and experience, but you, in the end, have to give them instructions on what you want done. They will tell you whether what you want to do is legal.

Architects

You may never need the services of a qualified architect, but you might need:

- *A professional survey of property you want to rent or buy*
- *Plans properly drawn up for local planning permission purposes. These might be necessary just for a sign on someone else's building or jutting out over the pavement.*

Banks and Building Societies

These are under one heading because they seem to provide similar services. However, for businesses they can be very different.

Building Societies which have become banks may allow a small trader or partnership to open a business account. Charges and services vary, so it is wise to shop around. You can open an account in your own name, or perhaps with one or two partners in private names, and use the account as though you were a private individual or individuals. If you do this, be sure to request that transactions are valid on one signature only. You would have to keep strict records showing that the money belongs to the company, and seek the advice of your accountant on tax returns.

All the major banks are very eager to help small businesses. They all have start-up packs, with help and advice on book-keeping procedures, banking procedures and so on. You are unlikely to have to pay bank charges during your first trading year.

Through your bank account you can deal with:

▶ *Standing Orders*
▶ *Direct Debits (including the monthly payment to the DWP for your National Insurance)*
▶ *credit transfers*
▶ *cheque payments with a company cheque (no cheque guarantee card)*
▶ *cash withdrawal (for Petty Cash purposes) by cash card.*

Make sure you get your bank statements at frequent intervals (monthly, not quarterly) so that you can keep your book-keeping up to date.

Your bank's small business manager will also be a good source of funding for the business if the case is properly presented (see Chapter 2) and will grant reasonable overdrafts to ease cash flow problems.

You can open a Deposit Account in your business name, and make arrangements for sums to be transferred to and from it as required. Your bank manager likes to see your money earning money.

On the payment side, after a year you will probably have to pay bank charges. Ask the bank for a breakdown of how these are calculated. If you arrange an overdraft, you will have to pay an arrangement fee – so the longer the arrangement, the better. Be sure to ask what the interest rates will be, and try to negotiate a lower rate if possible; these are not fixed charges.

If you are paid by a cheque which bounces ('Return to Drawer'), the onus is on you to:

▶ *instruct your bank not to re-present the cheque to your customer's bank*
▶ *chase the customer yourself.*

If you do not do this, your bank will go on re-presenting the cheque and charging you every time it does so.

Do not be misled into thinking that because you pay a cheque into your bank account at your own branch it will always be cleared on that day. It will often take two working days to clear. If, for example, you transfer money from your Building Society into your bank account and on the same day write a cheque which is presented on that day or the next, it could be that the cheque is processed *before* your transfer is credited to your account, and you will be charged interest on 'insufficient funds'. This can happen quite easily over a weekend.

Like a good accountant, a helpful bank small business manager can be a great asset, in spite of the charges which sometimes seem hidden to the unwary. Do ask this person for help and advice: many banks have people specially assigned to small business enterprises.

Estate agents

As already mentioned (see Chapter 3) there are usually estate agents who specialize in business premises. They will be able to advise you on:

- *what is available*
- *local developments*
- *local planning restrictions*
- *the size of premises which are right for your business*
- *the best locality for your business.*

They will also be able to draw up inventories for you, if necessary, on fixtures and fittings which are part of the purchase or lease of the property.

Generally speaking estate agents do not, at the present time, deal with conveyancing, leasing or rental agreements.

HM Revenue & Customs (VAT)

It might seem strange to list the VAT officer under 'Professionals', but in fact your VAT officer can be very helpful to you. As it says in Chapter 7, you may choose to become VAT registered, even if your turnover is under the limit of £68,000 per annum (2009 figures). Once you have decided to register, you cannot choose to become de-registered.

Your local VAT office can give very good advice on what is and is not liable to VAT, for both charging and claiming purposes, and what is zero-rated. They will also advise you on how you should show calculations on invoices, particularly where there is a mixture of VAT rates and complications such as discounts and carriage charges.

Insight

Visiting our local VAT office, we noticed a local trader unloading bundles of cash from his pockets and saying 'Just tell me what I owe you'. We can't help feeling this meeting should have been more private.

The VAT man has the right to enter your business premises (even when you work from home) at any time to check your books. Usually they make an appointment, and give you time to arrange to have your accountant with you if you wish. Like HM Revenue & Customs, if they find one mistake in your books, they are able to say that the Returns are incorrect, and go through everything with a fine-tooth comb. The VAT officers do not set out to be oppressive. They are strict and efficient but they are always willing to help, if asked.

Insurance brokers

Insurance brokers are the middle people between you and insurance companies; they do all the work of finding the right insurance policies for your needs.

Under the Financial Services Act, they are by law required to give you 'best advice'. Although they earn their money by being paid commission by the insurance companies, they should not recommend a particular company if that is not the best for you.

They should be able to advise you on the type of insurance you
need for your business, for example:

Buildings	Goods in transit
Contents	Your own life
Special cover	Loss of earnings through accident or illness
Vehicles	Professional negligence (doctors, lawyers, architects, counsellors, etc.)
Public liability	Employer's liability (if you employ others)

There are often brokers or insurance companies which specialize
in your type of business; you can probably get their names through
personal recommendation from other people in the same line of
business as yourself.

Insight
On-line insurance brokers (such as the many websites which
advertise on TV) are usually for private insurance. They
spend vast amounts of money on their advertising.

Printers

If you are not used to designing logos, letterheads, packaging and
other similar materials, you can seek the advice of a professional
marketing consultant (see Chapter 5). If you are starting off in a
very small way, ask your printer for advice.

Printers like to see their products looking good, and they have an
eye for these things. They can advise you on such things as:

▶ *quality, size and colour of paper and envelopes*
▶ *layout of letterheads*
▶ *size of typeface.*

Some printers run a start-up pack for small businesses, and
will provide you with a small amount of letterheads, envelopes,

business cards and compliments slips to get you started
(see Chapter 10).

A small printer is a good idea to begin with, because you will
not want more than about a ream (480–500 sheets) of printed
stationery in case you change your mind about your logo,
name and address etc. Larger printers tend to work on large
orders.

Printers often run a photocopying service and can recommend
secretarial services.

Office services

There is usually a word processing or office services bureau
somewhere in your area, or a professional working from home.
You can find them in *Yellow Pages*, Thomson or the Classified
Advertisements section of your local paper.

They will produce top quality letters, envelopes, labels,
reports, proposals, business plans. They should also check
and amend your English, if necessary, and even re-write or
compose letters, etc. for you; checking spelling and grammar
is generally part of the service, but re-phrasing or composing
will cost a little more. They will normally quote you per
A4 page or per 100 words: check whether this includes VAT
or not.

These bureaux will often run a photocopying service, which will
enhance the presentation of your work. This is important if you
want to make a good impression on someone like your bank
manager – it shows you mean business.

Office services will often include such facilities as telephone
answering, website maintenance, preparation of PowerPoint
presentations and book-keeping. If you cannot cope with all

the administrative work on your own, and cannot afford to employ anyone full or part-time, office services might be useful, particularly as your business expands.

Solicitors

Lawyers have a reputation for being slow. This is because they have to protect your interests and their own by being extremely thorough about every word they draft. A badly drawn document can cause untold misery. They also often have to deal with official bodies, such as local authorities, who are themselves slow to respond. If you need very quick action, make this clear to your solicitor; they can get things done very fast if necessary.

Solicitors often specialize in certain aspects of their work, such as litigation (court work) or housing. However, most firms will deal with basic legal work such as conveyancing, drawing up a lease, and so on.

A solicitor will advise you and draw up the appropriate documents for:

- *conveyancing*
- *leasing*
- *sub-letting*
- *rental agreements (for the rental/hire of plant, machinery, etc.)*
- *planning permission*
- *a partnership agreement*
- *employment law*
- *Memorandum and Articles of Association and more.*

There may be a Law Centre in your area which, if it cannot deal with your particular requirement, will advise you where to go to get the most cost-effective advice.

Solicitors should be able to give you a fairly accurate quotation for the work involved. Ask for this, so that you can budget accordingly.

Insight

Legal work usually takes longer than you think it will, so allow time for it.

CHECKLIST

Most of the professionals listed in this chapter are needed only occasionally. Your accountant and bank manager are important to you – choose them with care. The services professionals can offer are, among others:

▶ **Accountant:**
  ▷ *Book-keeping*
  ▷ *VAT returns*
  ▷ *Annual trading accounts*
  ▷ *Tax returns*

▶ **Architects:**
  ▷ *Property surveys*
  ▷ *Plans for planning permission*

▶ **Banks:**
  ▷ *Current account with cash card*
  ▷ *Deposit account*
  ▷ *Standing orders*
  ▷ *Direct debit*
  ▷ *Credit transfers*
  ▷ *Monthly statements*
  ▷ *Loans*
  ▷ *Overdrafts*

▶ **Building societies:**
  ▷ *Personal account services*

▶ **Estate agents:**
  ▷ *Property availability*
  ▷ *Local developments*
  ▷ *Planning and use restrictions*
  ▷ *Inventories*

▶ **HM Revenue & Customs (VAT):**
  ▷ *Making VAT returns*
  ▷ *What is and is not VATable*

- ▶ **Insurance brokers:**
  - ▷ *Type of insurance you need*
  - ▷ *The best policy or policies for you*

- ▶ **Printers:**
  - ▷ *Printed stationery*
  - ▷ *Advice on paper, letterheads, etc.*

- ▶ **Office services:**
  - ▷ *Word processing*
  - ▷ *Photocopying*
  - ▷ *Binding*
  - ▷ *Website design and maintenance*

- ▶ **Solicitors:**
  - ▷ *Conveyancing*
  - ▷ *Leasing and renting*
  - ▷ *Planning permission*
  - ▷ *Partnership agreement*
  - ▷ *Memorandum and Articles of Association*

10

The office

In this chapter:
- **Stationery:** *stationery suppliers*
- **Business documents:** *estimate; quotation; order; invoice; credit note; statement; remittance advice; letters, faxes and emails*
- **Computers:** *the materials; computer suppliers*
- **Telecommunications:** *telephones; fax; email; website*
- **Furniture and equipment**
- **Health and Safety at Work etc. Act 1974.**

Whatever your business, you need an 'office', even if it is only the corner of your dining table. You have to plan ahead to make sure you do not suddenly find you want to write a letter or send an invoice and you have no headed paper. You need to be systematic to keep your paperwork up to date. Although you will do most of your correspondence by email, you still need to write a formal letter occasionally.

Stationery

The stationery you are likely to need, depending on the nature of your business, is:

Headed paper For letters (at least 70 gsm, preferably 80 gsm in weight); gsm stands for grams per square metre

Plain paper Of the same weight and colour for continuation sheets

Unless you run a cash payment business:

Paper	For invoices, estimates, quotations: you can use your letterheads for all these, provided you give your document a definite name
Envelopes	Some good quality (the same weight and colour as your best paper); some manilla or white for run-of-the-mill correspondence
Labels	These are very useful for mailshots
Compliments slips	These are merely a piece of your good paper with 'With compliments' and your company name, address, telephone number, email and website printed on. They are very useful for slipping in with the odd bit of advertising material or invoice; you do not have to bother to type a letter, but you can handwrite a short message

NEWCO

22 ELMHURST ROAD   HAWTON   NORTHANTS   NN7 4PX
TELEPHONE 01327 563418   FAX: 01327 563520   VAT REGISTRATION: 987 6543 21
E-MAIL NEWCO@AOL.COM   WWW.NOOCO.CO.UK

With Compliments

| **Business cards** | Have some of these done early, and have them with you at all times |
| **Order book/bills** | Your business might require standard books of order forms or bills with carbon interleaved: these can be useful until you get your printed order forms and invoices organized |

You will need to think about the design of your stationery. Try to get it to match your company image – and colours, if you have any. It is worth getting some expert advice on this: printers have a wide experience of styles and colours and can be really helpful. However, you have to be careful that printers do not get carried away with their own enthusiasm and run you up very large bills. Some well-established printers prefer to do longer runs and charge a lot for very small orders. Some printers specialize in short runs – these are the ones you should try to seek out. Franchises such as Prontaprint can be a good place to start – they sometimes do a 'starter pack' just to get you under way (see Chapter 9).

If you can get a good master copy of your letterhead made, you can get the first batch of stationery (100–200 sheets) copied on a good photocopier. Make a master with your letterhead on it, and photocopy this onto your (coloured) quality paper. This is the sort of run that a professional printer will not want to bother with, and for which you could be charged more than is necessary. As soon as your style, address and amounts required are established, you can shop around and get all your printing requirements professionally produced, or produce it yourself on your desktop.

Things to remember to put on your letterheads:

- ▶ *company logo (if any)*
- ▶ *company name, address and telephone number*
- ▶ *fax number, email and website addresses*
- ▶ *VAT registration number (if any)*
- ▶ *names of proprietor, partners or directors (see Chapter 4).*

It is very important to keep copies of all your business documents.
Do a rough printout of your document to check that it is right,
or a photocopy of the finished product. A box of scrap paper
(all the printouts you reject or the unused sides of junk mail) is
useful for rough printouts. You can save reams that way, without
sacrificing the excellence of your image. It may seem fussy, but you
can lose a lot of your profit in wastage if you do not order and use
your stationery economically. Keep copies of emails or faxes as
necessary.

All business stationery and printing can be charged to the business,
and the VAT is reclaimable (see Chapter 7).

STATIONERY SUPPLIERS

You can get supplies of stationery from High Street shops,
but a stationery supplier is often more economical. You will
find these in *Yellow Pages* or your local *Thomson Directory* or
on the internet. What suppliers often do is use a standard
catalogue and fix their own prices; they sometimes have special
offers on standard stationery such as photocopying paper,
envelopes, toner cartridges, etc. There can be an enormous
difference in price, delivery facilities and payment terms, so it is
worth shopping around.

As a business, you can also use a cash and carry wholesaler such
as Bookers or Staples, but of course they do not deliver. However,
they are usually open until late at night and sometimes seven days
a week. You might already be intending to buy from a cash and
carry wholesaler, particularly if you run a small retail shop. If so,
remember the office side (in the non-foods area) as well.

It's also worth searching the internet: printer cartridges, in particular, are often perfectly OK, delivered the next day and cost a lot less. Make sure the cartridge, if not the manufacturer's own, is compatible with your printer and that your printer is not 'protected' so that it will work only with its own official manufacturer's cartridges.

Business documents

When you are laying out your business documents, make sure that each has all the information needed and, most important, the right name of the document. Call an estimate a quotation, and you could land yourself in trouble. Always remember to include your company name, address, telephone number, email and website addresses on every document.

> **Insight**
> Always leave more space above a sub-heading than below it, so that the sub-heading belongs to the text it refers to.

Different types of business need different documents, but here are descriptions and formats for the main ones. Look at the design and layout of the documents coming in to your business; this will help with the layout and design of your own.

ESTIMATE

(Ordinary headed paper will do.)

This is an *estimate*, as it says, of how much the service will cost. An estimate is not necessarily the final price to be charged. It is often used by businesses like builders and decorators who do not know what they might uncover as the job progresses.

Remember to say that VAT is extra – for instance *All charges subject to x% VAT*. Often *E & OE* (Errors and Omissions Excepted) is added at the bottom.

22 ELMHURST ROAD   HAWTON   NORTHANTS   NN7 4PX
TELEPHONE 01327 563418   FAX: 01327 563520   VAT REGISTRATION: 987 6543 21
E-MAIL NEWCO@AOL.COM   WWW.NOOCO.CO.UK

ESTIMATE

(today's date)

Mr R V Pugh
12 Ravens Close
Willington
Northants
NN7 6RL

          Estimate for redecorating outside of
               'Mountside' Hill Lane Andley

To: re-paint windows, doors and
      garden gate on the outside of
      the property in a colour to
      be selected.

                    for the sum of   £3,029
                         plus VAT

Please note:

If our estimate is accepted, work will be
started in one month's time.

QUOTATION

(Ordinary headed paper.)

A quotation gives a firm price for a product or service, again usually net of VAT. The layout can be the same as for an Estimate.

....
> ## Insight
> Customers tend to prefer to receive a quotation, rather than an estimate, naturally, because they know what they are getting. Make sure your quotation covers everything.
....

ORDER

(Printed or computer format needed.)

If you need your customers to place written orders for your product or service, you can provide them with an Order Form. This will make sure that you get all the details *you* need to fulfil the order correctly. Do not forget VAT, postage and packing or carriage and discounts, if these are applicable. You may wish to set up an Order Form on your website.

INVOICE

(Printed or computer format desirable, but can be typed on headed paper.)

These are the details which should always appear on an invoice (see example invoice on page 138):

1 *Name and address of supplier*
2 *Name and address of purchaser/customer*
3 *Date*
4 *Invoice number*
5 *Order number (if applicable) or reference*
6 *Quantity and description of goods (plus catalogue number if applicable) or service*
7 *Unit price*

22 ELMHURST ROAD   HAWTON   NORTHANTS   NN7 4PX
TELEPHONE 01327 563418 FAX: 01327 563520   VAT REGISTRATION: 987 6543 21
E-MAIL NEWCO@AOL.COM   WWW.NOOCO.CO.UK

ORDER

Date (today's date)
Order No 52879
To   Paper Supplies Ltd
         78 Church Road
         DARTFORD
         Kent
         DA12 6TU

QTY	DESCRIPTION	UNIT PRICE	£ PRICE
10	Boxes white photocopy paper	12.00	120.00
5	Reams blue photocopy paper	2.90	14.50
20	A4 lever arch files	3.75	75.00
50	A4 spiral pads	1.60	80.00
	Net		289.50
	VAT 17.5%		50.66
	Grand Total		340.16

① **NEWCO**

22 Elmhurst Road   Hawton   Northants   NN7 4PX
Telephone 01327 563418   Fax: 01327 563520   VAT Registration: 987 6543 21
E-mail Newco@aol.com   www.nooco.co.uk   ⑭

INVOICE

③ **Date** (today's date)   ④ **Invoice No** 2101
⑤ **Order No** 365
② **To**   Messrs P J Voyce and Partners
213 High Road
BURNLEY
Lancs BB1 2VW

DESCRIPTION	PRICE £
⑥ 40 copies Contract ⑦ @ £2.00 each Preliminaries	80.00
2 copies Final Contract @ £13.00 each	26.00
⑧ NET VALUE	106.00
⑨ **LESS** DISCOUNT AT 2.5%	2.65
	103.35
⑩ **PLUS** CARRIAGE	10.00
	113.35 ⑪
⑫ VAT AT 17.5%	19.84
⑬ INVOICE TOTAL	133.19

⑮ Terms 30 days net

8 *Total without VAT*
9 *Discount (if applicable)*
10 *Postage and packing, carriage (if applicable)*
11 *Final net total*
12 *Amount of VAT at appropriate percentage(s)*
13 *Total including VAT*
14 *VAT registration number*
15 *Payment terms*

Insight

NOTE The VAT is added after all the other calculations have been made.

CREDIT NOTE

(Printing and layout similar to an invoice.)

Sometimes if an order has not been totally fulfilled, the goods are unsatisfactory or a client has overpaid for some reason, you have to issue a credit note, stating the amount and the reason. Try to relate the credit note to your order number or invoice number – and remember to allow the customer the credit due on the next invoice or statement.

Insight

You may find a refund for unsuitable goods better than a credit note – the customer may never come back for another order, and the amount of the credit is likely to be different from the amount of the next order.

STATEMENT

(Printed or computer form desirable, but can be done on headed paper.)

Occasionally you have to render a statement of a customer's account – it is often a reminder to pay. Some companies make it a policy to pay only on receipt of a statement. If, through

22 ELMHURST ROAD   HAWTON   NORTHANTS   NN7 4PX
TELEPHONE 01327 563418   FAX: 01327 563520   VAT REGISTRATION: 987 6543 21
E-MAIL NEWCO@AOL.COM   WWW.NOOCO.CO.UK

STATEMENT

Statement date: (today's date)

To   Messrs P J Voyce and Partners
213 High Road
BURNLEY
Lancs BB1 2VW

Invoice date	Invoice number	DEBIT £	CREDIT £	Balance due £
(Date of Invoice)	2101	133.19		133.19

experience, you find out that a company adopts this policy, you should render the statement almost simultaneously with the invoice. Some companies render a document which they call an Invoice/Statement, and some send out Statements of Account automatically every month.

The statement should show the dates and numbers of outstanding invoices and details of totals without and with VAT. Details of the products or services need not be included – you have already given this information on the invoices. Some statements include the length of time the invoices have been outstanding, and any payments received during the statement period. Remember to date the statement.

REMITTANCE ADVICE

(Probably printed, attached to invoice or statement.)

When your customers pay you, it is useful for you if they fill in your own Remittance Advice (some companies make this a tear-off slip on the invoice or statement). Rather like the order, it gives you details which make the book-keeping easier at your end – the details on the Remittance Advice will be of your choosing, and may include your name, address and customer reference number, your customer's name and address, invoice number, date and totals without and with VAT.

The secret of all these documents is to have as few variables on each as possible – all you should have to do when sending the document out is to fill in details relevant to that particular customer. You should not have to fill in document name, your own company name and details, for instance, every time. Use a computer, or get the documents printed.

LETTERS, FAXES AND EMAILS

It is very important for your image to send letters, faxes and emails which are correctly typed and spelled and look good on the page. (See Chapter 5 for letterhead and email design.)

Try to address your communication to a named person or a job
title, if you are writing to a company ('The Sales Director', for
example). Communications addressed to the company only tend to
get shunted round from department to department. Identify quickly
what you are writing about by giving either a reference, or a
heading, or both.

A typical business letter layout is shown on page 145.

If you are in any doubt about spelling, grammar or sentence
construction, get someone to check it for you. All your
documentation should be to the high standard you set
yourself for the rest of your business operation.

Letters have evolved an etiquette for language and layout,
but email is still establishing itself in these areas. Follow these
suggestions, and your email will be acceptable to the reader:

Layout:

▶ *Subject: make the subject heading meaningful to the reader. If
your recipients don't know what the email is about, they are
less likely to open and read it*
▶ *If you don't know the reader it's better to start with
'Dear ...' than 'Hi!' Sign off with 'Regards' or, later,
'Kind regards'*
▶ *If you have several slightly different things to say, use
sub-headings, and make sure there is more space above
the sub-heading than below it. Use* **bold**, *not* CAPITAL
letters. Leave spaces between paragraphs
▶ *If you are writing about two totally different subjects,
send two emails. People often don't read to the bottom*
▶ *Take time to plan, so that the email is well constructed.*

Language:

- *If in doubt, use more formal language. It's not appropriate to write business emails in the language of text messages*
- *Don't key in words or sentences in all capital letters; people think you are shouting at them*
- *Do use initial capital letters for names and words like 'I'*
- *Check the spelling*
- *Don't use symbols and smileys, unless you know the reader very well*
- *Write good, correct, straightforward English – which isn't as easy as it sounds!*

Insight

If you are a limited company, your emails should be designed to incorporate all the details you have on your letterhead (company name, address, registration number, etc.).
You also need a disclaimer – see the Business Link website www.businesslink.gov.uk.

Computers

A desktop or laptop is a must for your business. Even if you are not computer literate yourself (and it takes time to learn how to use a desktop to the best advantage) a family member, business partner or employee will expect to work with a good machine. Businesses are expected to be able to send and receive emails and have their own website, but make sure your system can cope with a variety of attachments.

What will you get in a personal computer package, and what can you use it for? You should get:

Hardware: a keyboard, mouse, screen, disk drive and printer as well as the central processing unit (CPU) which makes the whole thing work.

The keyboard will be a normal QWERTY keyboard – so called because those are the first letters of the alpha keys on the top row – with extra function keys. Some will have a numeric keypad on the right, but you can always use the numbers on the top row of the keyboard proper. Remember to use the zero, not a capital 'O', for nought and a one, not a small 'l' (ell), for one. Check that your keyboard has a euro (€) key or access to the symbol.

The printer is the key to the quality of output. Get as good a printer as you can afford – a laser printer if possible.

Colour printers enhance the quality of the output for proposals and other 'selling' documents, and are becoming a must for all businesses.

The software: the computer programs, which allow you to control your computer and do things such as word processing, book-keeping and so on.

You could get:

- ▶ *A good word processing package, for correspondence, reports, etc. WP software is sophisticated and will meet most documentation needs*
- ▶ *An accounts package for book-keeping*
- ▶ *A spreadsheet, which you can use for doing cash flow forecasts, production forecasts, etc.*
- ▶ *A spellchecker for checking your spelling; they are not infallible because they often cannot cope with homonyms (their/there etc.). This comes as part of the WP package*
- ▶ *A 'presentations' package for creating graphs, slides, transparencies, etc.*
- ▶ *Communications software which (with the aid of a MODEM) will allow you to access email, the internet and send (and receive) faxes directly from your computer.*

Sometimes some or all these software packages are included with the hardware package you buy, but sometimes they come as extras. You need to check.

22 ELMHURST ROAD   HAWTON   NORTHANTS   NN7 4PX
TELEPHONE 01327 563418   FAX: 01327 563520   VAT REGISTRATION: 987 6543 21
E-MAIL NEWCO@AOL.COM   WWW.NOOCO.CO.UK

(Today's date)

Mr D Waverley
Customer Relations Manager
B & A Pyecroft Ltd
16 Southampton Row
LONDON
SE14 4ZW

Dear Mr Waverley

Document binding

We are pleased to announce a new service which we think will
improve the presentation of your work and enhance your
company image. Your important documents can now be bound in
plain, transparent or window covers in an attractive range of
colours.

For real impact and style your company name and logo
can be printed on the covers. The printing can be done in
black, blue or gold; choose the colour which best suits the
cover.

Please read our enclosed leaflet, which we are sure you will find
exciting. It contains not only a list of our charges, but also
illustrations of how your documents could look. It gives full
details of colours, sizes and styles, and our attractive
introductory offer on prices.

Try our new DOCUMENT BINDING service and present your
documents with pride.

Yours sincerely

Office Manager

Enc Leaflet

You always get at least one instruction manual *but* some are still incomprehensible to non-computer people. Sometimes you find word processing instructions which are 'idiot-proof' and accounting instructions which you cannot understand, all in the same manual. Again you need to check.

THE MATERIALS

As well as the system (hardware and software) you will need:

Cables	Sometimes part of the package, sometimes extra
Disks	As well as disks that make your desktop work (called system, operator or program disks), which will probably come with the desktop package, you will need some additional CDs on which to store or backup the work you do. There are two versions of these: CD-RW (ReWritable, which means you can delete or overwrite the data); CD-R (Readable, which means the data is permanently burned into the disk and cannot be amended).
Cartridges	For the printer
Paper	For special applications such as database printouts; for general purposes normal paper will suffice

There are lots of other 'extras' which you may or may not need. Look at a computer supplies catalogue if you want to see the sort of thing you can get. Remember anyway that you have to budget for at least the basics, which can cost quite a bit in both money and learning time.

COMPUTER SUPPLIERS

As with stationery, you can buy a desktop or laptop in many High Street shops, but it is worth going to a supplier who can advise you on what is best for you, and give you help when you need it initially. Computer manufacturers will usually be able to give you the name of your nearest supplier of their machines.

Take time to do some research before laying out capital on a desktop or laptop. Visiting a computer exhibition can be helpful, but try to go with someone who knows what to look for.

You might like to consider having a maintenance agreement for any of the larger systems. It is something to talk to your supplier about, because you become very machine dependent and can lose a lot of business if your system stops working for any length of time.

Insight

Go wireless. You might like, from the start, to set up your system as wireless, which means you can be keying-in in one room and printing in another, for example. No connecting cables are required.

Telecommunications

This is the word for any method of computerized communication between businesses, and includes telephones, fax, email, computer networks and so on. We shall deal only with telephones, fax, email and websites.

TELEPHONES

Obviously you will need a telephone, but will an ordinary telephone be enough? These are the alternative extras you could consider:

▶ *Plug-in extensions or small, modern PBX (private branch exchange) – which used to be known as the switchboard.*
▶ *Last number re-dial (press a button and the last number you dialled is automatically re-dialled).*
▶ *Loudspeaker and mike, so you do not have to use the handset, and everyone in the office can hear what is being said, and can join in.*
▶ *Memory for those numbers you use frequently.*

- ▶ *Mobile phone: it will probably be an essential part of your communications plan; it depends on how necessary it is to be able to get hold of you at all times. It might also ease family tensions if you can let the people at home know how late you will be and is a good personal security aid. Remember it is illegal to use a handheld mobile phone while driving.*
- ▶ *Voicemail or answering machine: this can be an integral part of the telephone terminal. It is useful to have one where you can pick up your messages from a distance, either voice or gadget activated. If you are offering a service, and the office is not always staffed, we consider an answering machine to be essential.*

FAX

This is short for facsimile; facsimile copies of documents can be transmitted almost anywhere in the world. The document is fed into the transmitting machine and sent via the telephone lines to the receiving fax machine. Machines are required at both ends of the communication channel, linked by a telephone line. Fax is very widely used; if your business is concerned with sending copies of documents to a large number of customers, a fax machine could be your next bit of telecommunications hardware after your telephone and answering machine, although most documents can be sent as attachments to emails.

Some machines incorporate fax, telephone, copier and answering machine all in one small unit, which means only one telephone line is needed. This could be ideal for the very small business.

EMAIL

Email is a must for most businesses, even very small ones. Create an email address for your business which is short, easy to use and incorporates some name allied to your business. Remember to include it on all your business stationery. If you are away from your desktop frequently, devise a routine for picking up your email messages regularly, and for accessing them from a distance.

WEBSITE

Use a website to market your business or to sell online. Make sure it is professionally designed and easy to maintain (see Chapter 5 and Chapter 14, the e-commerce chapter).

Furniture and equipment

FURNITURE

You can manage with very little purpose-built furniture to start with, but you should try to keep all your business documentation separate from your general household paperwork, if you are working from home.

You will find that you very soon need, at least:

▶ *Files in which to keep correspondence, copy invoices, etc.*
▶ *Somewhere to keep the files – probably a two-drawer cabinet will do to start with.*
▶ *Somewhere to store your stationery – desk drawers or a small cupboard are better than filing cabinet drawers.*
▶ *A table or desk for your desktop or laptop – make sure it is big enough to take the desktop and the papers you are working from.*
▶ *A chair of the right height for writing or keying. It may not be you who does the writing or keying, but whoever does it needs a desk or table and chair of the right height. This is very important, because working for any length of time at the wrong height can cause backache, wristache and all sorts of other aches and pains. It is worth getting an adjustable typing chair with good back support.*

There is usually a second-hand office furniture shop not too far away, from which you can get your basic furniture. Sometimes you can be lucky and hear of a large office which is being refurbished and needs to get rid of its out-of-date furniture. This can be quite prestigious furniture, but if you are working from home, make sure it will fit in!

If your business requires prestigious looking furniture from the start, remember to include the cost in your business plan.

EQUIPMENT

Items of equipment you may need are:

Stapler and staples
Hole puncher
Guillotine
Paper clips
Metal waste paper bin
Franking machine, if your business requires lots of mailshots
Sellotape
Scissors

Desk lamp(s): it is important to have good direct lighting on your papers, particularly if you are working with a desktop – light reflecting on the screen can give you eyestrain

Fireproof and smokeproof container for very important reference sources, like accounts books, and computer disks

A safe to keep money and valuable items, if yours is a retail business

Franking machine
If your postal output is sufficient to warrant it, you could use a franking machine. If you are a franking machine user, you have to:

▶ *obtain authority from the Post Office before starting to use a machine*
▶ *pay in advance for postage at a specified post office*
▶ *follow the local conditions about how to face and bundle franked mail*
▶ *return a completed control card to the Post Office at the close of business each working week*
▶ *use a machine authorized by the Post Office and have it regularly maintained.*

Photocopier
After a telephone and a desktop, a good photocopier is probably the next important item of equipment. Get as good a one as you can afford. These are some of the features to look out for:

▶ *automatic sheet feed*
▶ *double-sided copying*

- *collator*
- *reduction and enlargement*
- *memory for reduction and enlargement*
- *two-page separation, for copying pages of books or magazines (but watch the copyright laws) and A3 masters as two separate A4 sheets.*

Insight

We lease a large photocopier which will copy, scan, print, send faxes and collate. This means we are self-sufficient for all flyers, programmes, posters and display materials, which can be done as and when needed.

Large suppliers are always willing to lease you a photocopier, with integrated Maintenance Agreement. This can be advantageous from the accounting point of view (ask your accountant) and very important if your copier is going to get heavy wear – it is the one item of office equipment which always seems to be jamming or breaking down. If you lease, you have to remember that you pay a charge every time you press the button, as well as your quarterly leasing bill.

If you buy a copier outright, you have no leasing charges, but you might spend a lot in maintenance. It is possible to get a Maintenance Agreement for copiers which are owned – ask the manufacturers how to go about this. There is a second-hand market in photocopiers, but you usually do not know how they have been used or misused.

There are plenty of photocopier paper suppliers around, but if you use inferior paper you can find it never stops jamming, or takes through two sheets at a time. It is worth considering using the paper sold, or at least recommended, by the suppliers.

Health and Safety at Work etc. Act 1974

Many people forget that The Health and Safety at Work etc. Act 1974 (HASAWA) applies just as much in the office as it does in any other workplace. If you are on your own, health and safety in the office is important because you cannot afford to have accidents. If you are employing others, you have a legal obligation to make their working conditions healthy and safe.

Health and safety in the office is really common sense, but there are a few DOs and DON'Ts.

DO

- ▶ *Make sure the electrical wiring is in good condition*
- ▶ *Route wires and cables through conduit*
- ▶ *Have the right fire extinguishers handy and topped up – and know how to use them*
- ▶ *Have sensible arrangements for making hot drinks*
- ▶ *Observe the precautions for unjamming paper in the photocopier – some parts of the machine get very hot*
- ▶ *Lift heavy items (e.g. boxes of paper) properly*
- ▶ *Keep fire exits clear at all times*
- ▶ *Know what to do in the event of a fire*
- ▶ *Ensure any staff know the fire drill*
- ▶ *Have the first aid box in a handy place.*

DON'T

- ▶ *Leave cabinet and cupboard doors open*
- ▶ *Open more than one drawer of a filing cabinet at a time*
- ▶ *Leave cables trailing*
- ▶ *Leave piles of papers and files where people can trip over them*
- ▶ *Let jewellery and ties or scarves dangle in moving parts of equipment*
- ▶ *Carry things which are too heavy for you; get help, or use a trolley*
- ▶ *Stand on chairs – use steps*
- ▶ *Use adhesive sprays (like Spray Mount) in confined spaces without ventilation*
- ▶ *Smoke.*

WHAT ABOUT VDUS?

Prolonged use of VDUs (Visual Display Units – your screen) can cause many aches, pains and even permanent damage. There are various Health and Safety Executive publications on this issue, giving the latest research findings, advice and guidance. Call the Health and Safety Executive Infoline on 0845 345 0055. They publish a leaflet called 'Working with VDUs', available as an HSE publication which you can download off the internet from www.hse.gov.uk.

Pregnancy
There is a fear of birth abnormalities, but there is no firm evidence that VDUs are a health hazard to pregnant women. Radiation from VDUs (the equivalent to that from a hair dryer or an electric blanket) does *not* appear to be a cause of birth abnormalities.

Stress through fear of working with VDUs can cause problems, as can badly designed workstations. If you are pregnant and worried about working with VDUs, try to arrange for someone else to do the VDU work. If a member of your staff is similarly concerned, treat the matter sympathetically and make alternative arrangements.

Eyestrain
People do complain of eyestrain and headaches after prolonged use of VDUs, but there is no evidence that VDU use damages the eyes. It is much more likely that spectacles are not worn when they are needed, or that incorrect spectacles are worn (bi-focals can be a particular problem), or that workstation design and job content is at fault. If in any doubt at all:

▶ *Have your eyes tested by an optician*
▶ *Check the workstation design, particularly for glare*
▶ *Consider the job rotation and whether you are spending too long at the VDU without a break. VDU work is very concentrated, which in itself can cause stress and fatigue. The HSE recommend ten minutes break from the screen (i.e. doing something else) every hour.*

Design of workstations

Badly designed workstations are the most likely cause of aches and pains. Check the following:

- *Sufficient space on the worktop, with document holders if required*
- *The worktop is at the right height*
- *The printer is at the right height*
- *The chair is comfortable and adjustable for height and angle*
- *Lighting is sufficient to illuminate surfaces from which work is being copied*
- *Lighting should not be directed straight onto the screen whether it is sunlight or artificial light – it can cause glare*
- *Ambient lighting should not be too harsh*
- *Daylight needs extra directional lighting for dull days and blinds for very sunny days*
- *A comfortable working temperature is required*
- *Use anti-static mats, sprays, etc. if necessary*
- *A pleasing decor is helpful – if working towards a wall, make sure you look at something unobtrusive and restful*
- *Do not work facing a window*
- *Make sure you sit up straight with your back supported and with your hands at the right angle to the keyboard*
- *Adjust the brightness of the screen to suit your requirements.*

IN GENERAL

There is a lot of work involved in setting up the admin and office side of your business, which can sometimes seem like time ill spent. You cannot run an efficient business without a good administrative backup – for instance, it is no good selling the product or service if you cannot collect the money – so do not begrudge the time spent on getting the office right from the start.

If you are opening a shop, your office requirements, from the cash handling point of view, will be different (see Chapter 12).

CHECKLIST

▶ *Design logo.*

▶ *Get letterheads designed and artwork done.*

▶ *Design outgoing emails.*

▶ *Organize preliminary supply of stationery.*

▶ *Design documentation – invoices, order forms, etc.*

▶ *Decide on a desktop or laptop.*

▶ *Organize telephones and answering machine or voicemail.*

▶ *Get basic furniture.*

▶ *Organize preliminary filing system.*

▶ *Decide on photocopying method – own, buy, lease or outside.*

▶ *Get essential items of equipment (see list on page 150).*

▶ *Check layout of office for ease of working and safety.*

Telephone number for the Health and Safety Executive: Infoline
0845 345 0055. Website: www.hse.gov.uk.

11

Employing others

In this chapter:
- *Staff recruitment: preparation; advertising; selection and interviewing*
- *Pay: statutory sick pay; maternity rights and pay; parental leave; pensions; holiday*
- *Written particulars of employment: main requirements; dismissal; period of notice; redundancy; working hours; discrimination*
- *Insurance*
- *HASAWA: policy statement; accident book; first aid; flexible working*
- *Data Protection Act 1998*
- *Staff training: induction training; further training*

It is quite a big step to start employing other people when you have been running a business on your own or in partnership. Employing others is not nearly such a minefield as many fear, however. For one thing, it is not true to say that you cannot get rid of an employee who turns out to be totally unreliable or incompetent – you can.

If you set out to be a reasonable, fair and sensible employer, and follow the basic rules about employing others, you have nothing to fear. There are plenty of sources of advice on the law and your statutory obligations: these will be mentioned in this chapter.

NB The rules and basics on employment law are given as they stand at the time of publication.

Staff recruitment

The first person you employ is often a friend or a member of the family. How do you set about finding someone you do not know, and selecting the right person to suit you and your methods of working?

Insight

Choose someone whose skills complement yours. A clone of yourself won't expand the skillbase of your business. In Chester House Productions one of us does the writing while the other does all the computer work, design, website maintenance and so on. We make a good team.

PREPARATION

To make sure you get the right person for the job, you must know what you are looking for. It is advisable to draw up a Job Description, which outlines the job, and a Person Specification which gives you a profile of what you are looking for: those elements which are essential in the person you want to employ, and those which are desirable. A Person Specification could look something like this:

Person Specification

Job title: WP Operator/Clerk

	Essential	**Desirable**
Qualifications:	GCSE Maths/English or equivalent	NVQ Administration Level 2
	Good with figures	Experience of
	WP Exam	book-keeping
	Good telephone technique	
Practicalities:	Lives near	Driving licence
Personal qualities:	Can work without supervision; flexible	

ADVERTISING

When advertising in the local press or the Job Centre remember to include in the advertisement at least: job title and brief outline; location; pay; full- or part-time; any special skills, knowledge, experience and personal qualities required; how to apply; closing date.

> **Insight**
> You might need an office employee to use certain packages, such as PowerPoint or Sage. Remember to include this in your advert and explore their experience when you interview them.

Your advertisement must not discriminate on grounds of race, sex, disability, age or whether a person is married, single, gay and so on; you may put preferred ages but you risk losing good people. It is illegal to employ children under 13; children between 13 and school leaving age may be employed under certain conditions – they can be employed to do a paper round, for example. There is no upper age limit for employment and, with the abolition of the earnings rule, pensioners may now earn as much as they wish. Mature people often make very good employees, especially on a part-time basis.

Refer to the BIS and Business Link websites for good advice.

SELECTION AND INTERVIEWING

If you are looking for someone to run a small office and think that 'good with figures' and 'good telephone technique' are essential, you should have some way of testing this. As far as telephone techniques are concerned, you could get applicants to telephone for an application form and make notes of how they deal with you on the phone. 'Good with figures' sometimes requires a simple maths test – GCSE level Maths is not always a sufficient indicator. GCSE level English does not mean that someone is capable of writing a good, clear, business English letter.

You can learn quite a lot from the way people fill in an application form, so try to use one. The areas normally covered in an application for employment form are: name; address; date of birth; skills; qualifications; employment history; outside interests.

Ask applicants to complete the form in their own handwriting, so you can see whether they can write neatly, can spell correctly and so on, if this is important to the job. The previous work experience can also be very revealing: it can give you a good idea of whether a prospective employee can hold down a job for a sensible length of time, or whether he or she tends to flit from job to job. Explore any gaps (even of a few months) in the working history. It could be that the applicant has been in prison. This is not a good reason for rejecting an applicant out-of-hand, but you need to know. Look out for any discrepancies in the way the form has been completed – for example, does the stated age tie up with the date of birth? If people are less than truthful on an application form, they might be slightly less than honest in their employment. If you ask for 'hobbies' on the form, explore what applicants mean by their replies. For example, 'football': does this mean they play (in which case they are probably fit) or do they watch? For 'music', if they listen, that is different from playing an instrument, which requires perseverance and manipulative skills. If they play in a group, band or orchestra, it shows you they are used to working with others.

From the application forms, select perhaps three or four to interview. Reject at once any which do not fulfil the essential requirements, and reply to all those who apply, even if it is only to say no.

When you interview applicants, ask questions to get them talking about themselves and what they can offer you and why they want the job. Asking open questions – What did you do? Why did you …? How did you …? helps to get them talking about their skills, knowledge, experience and personality. Of course you should also make sure they understand not only what the terms and conditions of employment are, but also what the job entails. A Job Description for a WP Operator/Clerk could look something like this:

Job title: WP Operator/Clerk

1 *Deal with all incoming and outgoing mail and email*
2 *Answer the telephone*
3 *Write letters*
4 *Do the company's book-keeping*
5 *Pay wages*
6 *Undertake banking*
7 *Use the desktop or laptop*
8 *Any other job needed to keep the office running smoothly*

If you let prospective employees see at least a Job Description at the interview stage (or send one with the Application Form) they can decide whether they can cope with the job, and might weed themselves out at an early stage. If you discuss the Job Description at the interview stage, it will give you an opportunity to find out where any weaknesses lie and where training would be needed. Putting 'Any other job' can sound vague, but it does mean the employees, if they accept the job based on the description, agree to be flexible. Be aware that under the Data Protection Act comments written on application forms or interview notes could have to be shown to the applicant. They could also be used in evidence by an unsuccessful applicant who claims their failure to get the job was because of discrimination on the grounds of sex, race, age, sexual orientation, religion or belief and disability.

Insight

If you are interviewing several applicants, you can make a note on your interview papers to remind you who was which, but be careful not to make derogatory remarks. 'Wearing a blue jacket' is OK, but 'Terribly ugly' is not!

Use the interview fully so that each side can find out as much as possible about each other. It takes time, but it is time well invested. A good employee will stay with you and quickly become part of the company. Employees who do not fit in leave, and then you have to start all over again.

Once you have made your selection, made a formal job offer in writing to the successful applicant, and have had a definite acceptance in writing, write to those who were not successful.

Insight

Good, well-chosen employees stay with you for a long time. Casually employed people can be apt to leave at short notice, and you have to start again, which is an expensive waste of time.

Pay

The amount of gross pay, plus overtime rates if applicable, will have been agreed between you at the interview/job offer stage. It is also useful to agree at that early stage:

▶ *The method of payment (straight into bank account or building society by credit transfer, cheque or cash)*
▶ *The frequency of payment (weekly or monthly).*

From an employer's point of view it is much less of a security risk to pay straight into an account by credit transfer. It is also more economical to pay monthly rather than weekly, because you usually pay in arrears, so you have the use of that money for about three weeks. An employee might wish to be paid weekly in cash. You, as the employer, must make up your mind what you are prepared to do and stick to it. You can ask an employee to change once he or she has started work, but it is better to lay down conditions of employment at the start.

As an employer you are committed to pay the employee the amounts and on the terms agreed which must not be below the national minimum hourly rate (see the BIS website). You must pay this, no matter what state the business is in.

You also have to make statutory deductions from the gross pay. These are:

▶ *Income tax*
▶ *National Insurance – employee's contribution.*

The employer's contribution is paid over and above the agreed wage of the employee, and is a percentage of that figure.

For all details of deductions, how they should be collected and how and when paid to the authorities, tax tables and so on, ask the DWP and HM Revenue & Customs. ACAS also do a very helpful leaflet called 'Employing People in the Small Business'. You can get this from the Job Centre.

You must supply the employee with the following:

▶ *Detailed wage/salary slip showing the gross pay, all deductions and the net amount payable. It does not matter if the slip is handwritten, but it must be given with the pay*
▶ *An annual P60 showing the amount of tax deducted in that financial year. This is the government's financial year from 6 April to 5 April, not the company's financial year*
▶ *If the employee leaves your employment, a P45 showing the amount of tax deducted to date in that financial year.*

Your accountant can advise on this.

STATUTORY SICK PAY (SSP)

As an employer, if your employee falls sick and is away for up to three working days, you do not have to pay them, but if he or she is off sick for four or more days, you must pay the employee sick pay, instead of a wage, for up to 28 weeks. You can get a rebate from the government if you keep details of people off sick, otherwise you have to pay for this. There are strict rules about how much must be paid, when and to whom, and about doctors' certificates. Ask your local DWP for details and for help if you are having to do this for the first time, and keep records. Other than SSP there is no legal requirement to pay employees who are off sick.

MATERNITY RIGHTS AND PAY

A pregnant woman has four statutory rights:

1 *Time off with pay for ante-natal care: she does not need to have worked for you for a specific length of time*
2 *Statutory Maternity Pay if she has worked for you for at least 26 weeks up to the 15th week before the expected week of confinement (EWC). You can claim this back*
3 *The right to maternity leave with maintenance of all benefits except pay*
4 *The right to return to work after maternity leave if she wishes*

There are detailed rules about managing maternity leave and pay and returning to work. Ask the DWP for details on all these points.

PARENTAL LEAVE

Both parents of a baby have the right to unpaid leave to be taken before the child's 5th birthday (or 18th birthday if the child is disabled). See the BIS website for guidance notes. New fathers who have been employed with you for a certain length of time are entitled to leave paid at the minimum statutory rate. This can be recovered from the Department of Work and Pensions, www.dwp.gov.uk. For information on paternity rights visit www.tiger.gov.uk.

PENSIONS

There is no legal duty to operate an occupational pension scheme, but once an employer has five or more employees, they must introduce arrangements for a Stakeholder Pension (see government website www.opra.gov.uk). The normal age of retirement must be the same for both men and women.

HOLIDAY

All employees are entitled to paid holiday. Part-time workers accrue their entitlement pro-rata. For details on how the minimum holiday rules operate, see the BIS booklet *A Guide to the Working Time Regulations* or check out the BIS website.

> **Insight**
>
> If you know your administrative skills are weak, it might pay you to employ a book-keeper to cover this area of your business, while you do the things you are good at. We have always 'done the books' ourselves, but it is our policy not to employ people. We have 'associates' instead.

Written Particulars of Employment

An employer is obliged, within two months of an employee starting the job, to give an employee written Particulars of Employment. There should be two copies of the document, signed by both parties – one copy to each.

This statement may be set out in one comprehensive document or it may be provided in instalments. However, the first eight items on the list must be contained in a single document:

1 *Names of employer and employee*
2 *Start date of employment*
3 *Start date of employee's period of continuous employment*
4 *Rate of pay and how it is calculated*
5 *Hours of work, including normal working hours*
6 *Holiday entitlement*
7 *The employee's job title (or brief description of work)*

8 *Place of work*
9 *Pension arrangements*
10 *Sick pay arrangements, if any*
11 *End date of employment (for short-term contracts)*
12 *Period of notice*
13 *Grievance and disciplinary procedures*
14 *Overseas employment information*
15 *Particulars of collective agreements which directly affect the employee's terms and conditions.*

See the ACAS website for details of their helpful booklets on contracts, handbooks and procedures: www.acas.org.uk.

DISMISSAL

> **Insight**
> Some people think it's impossible to dismiss staff, but that isn't true, provided you have good grounds for doing so and follow the correct procedures.

You can dismiss people for:

incompetence; misconduct; redundancy; retirement; special circumstances (for instance loss of driving licence if a driving licence is essential to the job); any other substantial business reason

You can dismiss people who have up to one year's service with the company without a reason. If you have dismissed a pregnant woman or someone with over one year's service, you are required to give one of the above reasons, in writing, for the dismissal.

In all circumstances it is essential to follow a disciplinary procedure.

1 *Verbal warning (noted in book)*
2 *Written warning*
3 *Final written warning*

Instant dismissal for a grave offence, like proven theft, is legal. The point of the legislation is to ensure that people are not dismissed out-of-hand for no good reason and without a fair hearing. An employer must:

- ▶ *Give a written note of the issues*
- ▶ *Allow a fair and unbiased hearing*
- ▶ *Listen to mitigation*
- ▶ *Allow the employee to be accompanied by a colleague or accredited trade union official*
- ▶ *Give the right of appeal, even if the appeal is to the person who took the decision in the first place.*

Provided you deal with your employees fairly, and with understanding, you should not fall foul of the law. It is worth documenting all that happens very carefully, in case you have to answer to an Employment Tribunal. Again ACAS publishes helpful booklets on this. An unfairly dismissed employee may be reinstated or awarded compensation to be paid by the employer.

PERIOD OF NOTICE

These are the minimum periods of notice an employer must give to an employee:

- ▶ *Up to one month's service – none*
- ▶ *Between one month's and two years' service – one week*
- ▶ *After two years – one week's notice for each complete year of service until (s)he has more than 12 years' service, when the minimum notice period remains at 12 weeks.*

An employee can leave without notice during the first month of service. After that an employee has an obligation to give at least a week's notice. Longer periods for both parties are normally written into the Particulars of Employment. Notice must be paid, even if you ask the person to leave before the end of the notice period.

If you retire an employee you must give them six months' notice of the date of their retirement and their right to ask to continue working after normal retirement age (which should not be less than 65). Refer to the BIS website for details www.bis.gov.uk.

REDUNDANCY

It is unlikely that you will get into a redundancy situation in the early years of the business. Redundancy occurs if, for some reason, the job no longer exists, and therefore you have to end someone's employment.

There are rules about redundancy and redundancy payments which you can obtain from the BIS.

WORKING HOURS

The Working Time Regulations 1998 impose rules on total weekly working hours, limits on night work, health assessments, rest periods, breaks and annual holiday. See the BIS booklet and website for helpful examples and guidance.

DISCRIMINATION

You must make sure you have equal pay and benefits for equal work (pro-rated for part-timers); you must not discriminate on grounds of sex, race, age, sexual orientation, religion or belief and disability in any aspect of employment; and sexual harassment can also be found to be discriminatory by an Employment Tribunal.

Insurance

As well as insurance on buildings, contents, public liability and possibly professional negligence, as an employer you have to have Employers' Liability Insurance, and display the Insurance

Certificate where employees can see it. Your Insurance Broker (see Chapter 9) should be able to advise you.

HASAWA

As an employer, you have a common duty of care towards your employees. The Health and Safety at Work etc. Act 1974 and a range of workplace health and safety regulations require all employers, self-employed people and employees not to put themselves or anyone else (contractors or visitors for instance) at risk.

Employers have an additional responsibility to ensure that the working environment (including offices) will not be detrimental to the safety and health of employees, contractors and anyone else working on their premises. This includes safe systems, storage, materials and machinery, as well as proper fire precautions, access and procedures.

You should assess all potential risks in your workplace, take reasonable precautionary measures, train people regularly in the procedures and monitor any changes. Training in the use of VDUs and lifting techniques is particularly important. There are additional obligations to protect new or expectant mothers, including a specific assessment.

Your workplace should be clean, and properly ventilated, lit and heated.

POLICY STATEMENT

If you employ five people or more, you are obliged to draw up a Health and Safety Policy Statement, and display it where every employee can read it. If you have over 20 employees, you have to have a Fire Certificate.

ACCIDENT BOOK

You are also obliged to keep a record of all accidents – normally in an Accident Book. An entry in the Accident Book must show:

▶ *name, sex, age, occupation of victim*
▶ *nature of injury and place where it occurred*
▶ *description of circumstances.*

For full details of regulations, see the HSE booklet.

FIRST AID

Higher risk workplaces must have a qualified first aider on the premises. For lower risk workplaces you do not need a first aider until you have 50 employees, and for medium risk workplaces 20 employees. However, it is sensible, if possible, to have someone who can administer first aid.

At the very least you should have a first aid box, easily accessible and regularly topped up. For details of what the box should contain, plus a full clear description of what to do, see the *First Aid Manual*, published jointly by The British Red Cross Society, St John Ambulance Brigade and St Andrew's Ambulance Association, obtainable from bookshops. Check whether you are permitted to dispense medication of any sort.

FLEXIBLE WORKING

At the moment only certain employees have the right to request a flexible working arrangement, but more and more organizations are extending the offer to all or part of their workforce. Legislation has recently been extended to include more of the working population.

Data Protection Act 1998

This Act applies to data held electronically (on computer, even if it is only a desktop or laptop) and manual data such as handwritten or typed records which are held in a filing system.

If you have processed any personal data about your employees beyond just names and addresses – for instance, if you have personnel information about rates of pay, domestic circumstances and so on – you must register with the Information Commissioner but be wary of bogus registration agencies.

Your employees have a right to know what personal data is being held, and whether it is correct. In practice, this means that most employers give their employees a printout of the information held once a year, and ask them to confirm or update it.

If you are using personal data purely for personnel reasons with your company you are unlikely to have problems. Problems arise when you use or disclose that data for some other purpose (selling employee lists to a marketing company, for example).

Here again, provided employers go about their business in a normal, straightforward and fair way, they should not fall foul of the law. For further details see the Information Commissioner's Office website www.dataprotection.gov.uk.

Staff training

Staff training is not necessarily about sending people away on courses, although this might be required sometimes. Staff training is about making people efficient and productive and enabling them to enjoy doing their work because they do it well. Most staff training can be done at the place of work.

INDUCTION TRAINING

Induction training should cover all a new employee needs to know fairly quickly, although not necessarily all on the first day. It should include:

- ▶ *whereabouts of facilities (toilet, kettle, etc.)*
- ▶ *security of personal possessions*
- ▶ *break times and what people normally do*
- ▶ *fire precautions and procedures*
- ▶ *introduction to colleagues*
- ▶ *whereabouts of materials, equipment, etc. needed for the job*
- ▶ *basic job procedures*
- ▶ *basic company rules, regulations and customs*
- ▶ *someone to turn to.*

It is time-consuming to train new people, but it is better than leaving them to dive in at the deep end. Make a checklist that you and the new employee can work from.

FURTHER TRAINING

It is usually not enough to show learners once only how to do something, and then expect them to do it to full Experienced Worker Standard (EWS). Try to train people in what to do a little bit at a time, and to follow this sequence:

1 Explain	**Tell** the learner not only what is to be done, but why and how it fits in to other jobs
2 Demonstrate	**Show** the learner how to do the job – slowly
3 Try out	**Let** the learner do the job while you are still there to watch
4 Correct	**Put right** any mistakes early on – bad habits are difficult to correct later. This is particularly important where safety is concerned

People need training and re-training all their working lives as laws, systems, machinery and equipment change. Allow your staff the time and facilities to keep up to date.

CHECKLIST

▶ Recruitment:
  ▷ *Draw up Job Description and Person Specification (essential and desirable).*
  ▷ *Design advertisement.*
  ▷ *Sift incoming applicants.*
  ▷ *Interview only a few, with Job Description.*
  ▷ *Write to successful applicant(s).*
  ▷ *After job accepted, write to unsuccessful applicants.*

▶ Pay and conditions:
  ▷ *You must pay agreed pay by agreed method at correct time; SSP, if applicable; maternity pay, if applicable.*
  ▷ *You must deduct NI and income tax.*
  ▷ *You must provide employees with a breakdown of pay and deductions; an annual P60; a P45, if applicable; written Particulars of Employment; Employer Liability Insurance cover.*

▶ Health and safety (HASAWA):
  ▷ *You must do your best to ensure healthy and safe working conditions; record all accidents; display the company's health and safety policy, if you employ five people or more; have adequate fire precautions and procedures.*
  ▷ *You should ensure someone knows about first aid; keep an adequate first aid box.*

▶ Data Protection Act:
  ▷ *You must register as a data user if you keep personal details; allow employees to examine and update their own records.*

▶ Staff training:
  ▷ *Make an Induction Training Checklist.*
  ▷ *Allow time and facilities for further training.*

12

....

Opening a shop

In this chapter:
- *Siting*
- *Image*
- *Stocktaking*
- *People*
- *Legal requirements*
- *Money*
- *Security*
- *Advertising*

Siting

RIGHT FOR THE MARKET

In deciding where your outlet should be sited, it is useful to ask yourself whether what you are offering is largely something which customers will buy on impulse if they happen to see it, or whether it is something they need, so will seek you out, within reason, wherever you happen to be.

This means you have two broad categories from which to choose – prime sites and secondary sites.

PRIME SITES

A prime site is where you will find the 'big boys', the household names which customers expect to find in any worthwhile shopping venue.

Prime sites are expensive, and a question you need to ask yourself is, 'If I choose a unit in a prime site, will people passing my door on their way to the branches of the national multiples be tempted to stop and consider my wares – and will they do it in sufficient numbers to justify the expense?'.

SECONDARY SITES

Secondary sites are located away from the prime site areas. Naturally the outgoings on a secondary site are lower than those for a prime site. The level of trade could well be lower, too, so you will probably need to tell the public that you are there, which means that advertising costs for a secondary site could be greater than those for a prime site. Many small shops site themselves on the periphery of a small town.

POSITION

Whether prime or secondary, it is worth considering the position of your outlet. For example, would you want to be actually fronting onto the street with pedestrians and traffic passing by or would you prefer to be within a shopping centre?

In considering a site it might be worth seeing who your neighbours will be. What type of goods will they be offering? Will they be in direct competition with you? Will they attract people who might equally be interested in what you have to offer?

SIZE AND SHAPE

Two units with the same square footage could offer good or bad possibilities depending on the shape and the type of stock to be fitted into it. So before tramping off to the agents or around the town centres, consider:

- ▶ *the optimum size of the unit you need (do not forget stockroom and office space as well)*
- ▶ *the most appropriate shape for the type of business you are intending to run.*

For example, a deep, narrow shop with very little frontage would be acceptable for a counter service operation – like a jeweller's or a motor accessories shop – but would be unsuitable for a self-service shop – like a mini-market – where customers need more space to walk around selecting their own items.

Decide how far either side of the 'ideal' you are prepared to go, and try to stick to it.

RENT AND RATES

The shape as well as the size of your unit will have an effect on the expenses. This is because of the way the rental is calculated. The floor area of the shop is divided into zones, with each zone attracting a different level of rent; the zone nearest the front of the shop being the most expensive, so that the rent for a deep, narrow-fronted shop is less than for a shallow, wide-fronted one.

PUBLIC TRANSPORT AND PARKING

Customers need to be able to get to and from your shop easily and conveniently, whether by public transport or under their own steam. When deciding on the siting of your potential outlet, ease of access for customers is something else to consider.

Insight

When weighing up the pros and cons of a particular site, pretend you are a customer. Try to park and find out where the buses stop, then walk to your proposed shop, stop and examine the outside of your shop and that of your potential neighbours. Go round the back, if you can, to see whether customers could pick up their purchases at the back door, particularly if you sell large items.

ACCESS FOR DELIVERIES

As well as thinking about how convenient it is for your customers to get to your store, it is as well to take into account how your stock will be delivered to you in the first place.

For any potential site, see what access there is for suppliers' or carriers' vehicles, and how easy it is to transfer items from a vehicle to your goods-in area.

THE COMPETITION

Consider whether it would be to your advantage to open up a shop opposite an existing outlet which sells a similar range of goods to you:

Advantages	Customers can easily make comparisons between outlets offering similar goods; you can highlight your business with special offers or other features which the competition is not doing
Disadvantages	Customers continue to support the existing outlet through force of habit; competitors can anticipate your opening, and mount their own campaigns to distract attention from you in those critical early days

You might then think it wise to set up amongst outlets which offer goods different from those you are planning to sell, so that you are, in effect, the sole supplier in that particular locality.

Image

The general image or impression that a retail outlet presents to the public at large depends on a number of factors, any of which, if not up to standard or of the wrong sort, can damage the overall effect. Even opening hours can contribute to the image of a business by giving an idea of the degree of service available.

PERSONAL SERVICE OR SELF-SERVICE

Once upon a time pretty well everything was sold across the counter, it was the accepted way of doing things. Those days are long gone, although the craze for throwing out counters and going over entirely to self-service has now diminished, and it is more usual to find a mixture of these methods.

Whenever self-service is used in an outlet, whether wholly or in part, it is always necessary to have somebody available at the cash point to handle customers' purchases. This person can be involved in other duties, but must always be alert to the needs of customers at the cash point, because the essence of the self-service system is convenience, and your image could be damaged if customers were kept waiting unnecessarily at the cash point for someone to take the money for their goods.

FIXTURES AND FITTINGS

The way your stock is presented to customers will depend a great deal on the type of fixture you are using. If you are taking over a unit you might well feel that you can make do with the fixtures left by the previous occupier. If yours is quite a different type of business, though, it might not be a wise decision if it means your stock is not shown off to the best advantage. Perhaps a slight adaptation will do the trick, but it could be a false economy if you are not doing justice to your stock.

A basic requirement of any fixture is that it is appropriate to the type of stock it is meant to hold. It needs to be secure, functional and easy to re-stock. Some fixtures are made to store backup stock in drawers or cupboards which makes re-stocking easy and convenient.

DECOR AND LIGHTING

Outward appearances are important to a retail outlet. Look at the various styles of decoration used by businesses, as well as the variety of colour schemes and try to decide what would be the most suitable decoration for the outside of your premises.

Having made the premises look attractive and inviting from the outside, you must continue that appeal into the interior. Do your research again, and see what other people do, particularly in your line of business.

A very important aspect of your internal decorations is the lighting. This really is an area which needs to be considered carefully: consider level of lighting, type of lighting (fluorescent, spot, and so on), direction of lighting and use of natural light.

RANGE OF STOCK

Stock is money, and stock on the shelves is money waiting to be transferred to the cash register drawer. You must invest money in stock or you will not have anything to sell, though of course it is not simply a case of getting hold of some stock lines and hoping for the best.

Whatever type of retail business you intend to run it is necessary to have a carefully-considered range of stock, sufficient to offer customers a suitable choice. Getting the balance right is the key; there must not be so much as to be confusing, nor yet too little for the choice to be unreasonably restricted.

So, do you try and go for the image of:

▶ *having whatever customers are likely to want, or*
▶ *satisfying the majority, leaving the minority customers to seek satisfaction elsewhere, or*
▶ *specializing, and catering for the minority?*

The contribution which stock makes to the image of your business should not be underestimated. Being the prime means of generating your profit, it makes sense to use it to create a favourable image for your business.

SUPPLIERS

What have suppliers to do with image? A simple answer to that question must be, a lot. It is your suppliers on whom you rely to see that you receive that all-important stock we have just been thinking about.

What you are looking for in a supplier is a reliable service, a continuity of supply and an acceptable range of lines. Unless you can get these, your image is going to suffer with your customers when they keep finding you are out of stock of the lines they want to buy, particularly the popular ones.

When sourcing suppliers take these points into account:

1 *Visit trade fairs and surf the internet*
2 *Find out who your competitors are using*
3 *Will you deal direct or through agents?*
4 *Take heed of recommendations by (friendly) competitors*
5 *Take trips abroad and visit UK suppliers*
6 *Be aware that some suppliers require minimum orders*
7 *Some suppliers may require the first payment up front because you have little or no trading history*
8 *Factor in the carriage costs.*

OPENING HOURS

Insight
It is almost impossible to run a shop entirely on your own – you need someone to cover for you.

The trend is for retail outlets to be open for six-day trading and in some businesses for seven. This arrangement might not be quite so easy for you if you are working on your own. Alternatively you might close for half a day according to local custom, or as dictated by local bye-laws. If your unit is situated within a shopping centre, your opening hours will be governed by the rules of the establishment.

Whatever the situation, you must make sure that your opening hours enhance your image rather than detract from it. Your image must be that you are there and open for business when customers want to spend their money.

Consider your opening hours carefully. If you state on your shop window (and you must put an 'opening hours' notice in the window or door) that you open at 9.00 am, then you must open at 9.00. If you don't, customers will go elsewhere.

Stocktaking

Stocktaking is an exercise to establish a current record of stock in hand at any given time. This is necessary, not only to establish the number of items, but also the cash value.

Stocktaking is a task undertaken at least once a year for the inclusion of the stock in the annual accounts. In practice a full stocktaking could well be done twice yearly or even quarterly. It is possible that in certain sections within a shop, stock would need to be taken weekly, or, in the case of very perishable items, daily, to provide the basis for an effective stock and order system.

We are concerned here, though, with the general stocktake. Accuracy is paramount for a stocktaking exercise. It is not a job to be rushed or fitted in between other things; it needs full concentration to get it right. This is why, very likely, you will find yourself doing this job out of trading hours, or at a weekend if the shop is closed.

The overall rule to follow for a successful stocktake is for everything to be methodical – the preparation, the execution, the follow-up.

PREPARATION

Have the sheets you intend to use for the stocktaking clearly identified – at least numbered in sequence. Make sure all are accounted for both before and after the stocktake.

The method you use to record your stock will depend on the type of business you have. In some cases you will write out a description of the item together with the selling price (retail stock is generally recorded at selling price), or it might be more suitable simply to head the record sheets with prices, and fill in the numbers of the items under the appropriate headings.

It is vital to mark in some way the areas which have been counted to avoid sections being missed or counted twice – a simple chalk mark on the floor or fixture might be sufficient.

FOLLOW-UP

When the counting has been completed, make sure all the stocktaking sheets have been collected in and are accounted for.

The graft of counting all the figures and arriving at a grand total for the value of the stock has now to be done.

Insight

Good, computerized stock and order systems are a great asset. Your stock level is automatically adjusted every time you sell an item. However, this doesn't account for stolen or damaged items, so a physical stocktake is still necessary. A shop in our locality which sells low-priced dresses finds that customers rip the dresses off their security tags to try them on, and then leave the dresses on the floor.

People

People form an important part of a retail outlet. How many people you will need in your shop will relate to your pattern of trading. You will need to consider whether to use all full-time staff, or perhaps supplement these with part-timers for peak trading times.

You will need to decide how your staff will be dressed; whether they will be provided with a uniform, or whether ordinary everyday clothes will be suitable – is suitable formal or casual? What will you be wearing?

Insight

If you happen to sell jewellery, clothing or other fashion items, make sure you and your staff wear something which goes along with that image. But remember you'll be on your feet all day, so don't go overboard on the shoes.

The hours of work will relate both to trade and financial considerations. Remember there is more to paying staff than just wages; for instance, you are responsible for NI contributions.

You will need to devise suitable conditions of employment for potential members of staff. These will include the type of facilities you will need – or would be prepared – to provide, such as toilet and washing facilities, a cloakroom locker, providing suitable security for personal belongings, and refreshment facilities, even if it is only for making tea or coffee.

Legal requirements

Many of the legal aspects of employing staff are dealt with in Chapter 11. In addition, when running a shop you should know the provisions of:

▶ *The Trades Description Act*
▶ *Sale of Goods Act*
▶ *Offices, Shops and Railway Premises Act*
▶ *Consumer Protection legislation*
▶ *Local bye-laws*
▶ *Fire prevention requirements.*

All the legislation is drafted to make sure shopkeepers sell goods which are of 'merchantable quality', properly described and at a price which is fair to the shopkeeper and the consumer.

If you do not know the necessary details of the law relating to keeping a shop, contact the Trading Standards Officer for your local authority.

The Fire and Rescue Service will advise you on what you must do to qualify for a Fire Certificate for your premises.

Insight

Many years ago a Fire Service video showed, for real, staff in an upstairs room of a large store, trying to get out as a fire raged on the ground floor. The windows had security bars across them, and hands thrust out through the broken window panes and through the bars told the story.

You will need to have third party insurance for your staff and customers – consult an insurance broker who specializes in small shops.

Money

A retail shop, by its very nature, is bound to be involved in money. You will need to consider how best to handle cash, cheques and debit and credit cards at the point of sale, including the chip and PIN system. This will require a set procedure to be devised, and it is important that everybody involved keeps to the system. For this to happen it would probably be helpful to have your procedure written down.

Taking money at the cashpoint can be a good opportunity to record those details which can provide useful management information, for example, by dissecting sales into suitable groups either by product, department or section. This will be a simple and effective way of creating data for management control, such as the basis for a stock and order system.

At certain times money will need to be banked. Establish a regular routine for this, but preferably not a regular route to and from the bank premises. We will consider this further in the next section – *Security*.

The two essential elements for this task are the preparation of moneys for banking, and the recording of banking transactions. The underlying requirement for this is accuracy. For this to be achieved, once again a definite procedure or system must be established and conscientiously followed by all concerned.

Security

Security should be a continual theme in all aspects of business activity. In this section we will consider four important areas: staff, stock, money and premises.

STAFF

Insight

Unfortunately, staff pilferage can be a major source of loss if not prevented. One very simple precaution: do not allow staff who handle cash to have their handbags or wallets anywhere near the cashpoint. In any case, these valuable items of personal property should be securely locked away.

It is useful to instil into all members of staff that they should be security-minded, in relation to the stock and moneys of the business as well as their own personal belongings. Try to make them realize that it is as much in their own interest as it is for the business always to be alert to situations where security is not all it might be. Encourage staff to come to you about any apparent lapses in security procedures, and with ideas for improving security arrangements – be sure to be receptive when they do. Security is an important subject which concerns every member of staff in some way or another – it helps if they are aware of this.

STOCK

The security of stock should be a continuous and conscious process. In the sales area, apart from stock actually on display, remember security includes accurate ringing up of prices, and being aware of the various dodges which can be used by customers for taking stock items past a cashpoint without paying for them. For example, taking items through in their own bags, hiding items in pockets or under coats, switching low-priced tickets onto high-priced items, not completely clearing a wire basket or trolley, are all methods used by customers to avoid payment.

In the storage area the accurate checking in of deliveries of stock is a very important part of stock security: a business cannot afford to pay suppliers for items of stock it actually never received.

If your shop is likely to handle highly pilferable items – perhaps lines which are small in size but high in value – then consider the best arrangements you can make for their security, for example, a locked security cage in the security area, and keeping them behind glass or behind the counter in the sales area. Perhaps alarmed wires threaded through stock items in the sales area, as often seen on displays of hi-fi equipment, etc., could be effective.

MONEY

Security and money would seem naturally to go together. Once again, there are various situations to consider, and to decide on set procedures or systems to meet them.

The simple device of making sure the cash register drawer is kept open for the least possible time, and certainly firmly shut between the end of one customer's order and starting the next, is a good security system to adopt.

Where cash is stored, security should be as effective as possible. Even if you cannot run to a separate 'custom-built' cash office, try to ensure that the area is as secure as possible during the time that cash is actually being handled and stored.

Whatever the situation, you will need some form of safe; take advice on this from your local Crime Prevention Officer. Incidentally, you have to remember floor loadings when considering the installation of a safe, the floor has to be strong enough to hold it; safe companies will no doubt be pleased to advise you.

We mentioned earlier that we would consider the security aspects of banking. Decide how you are intending to transport moneys to and from your bank. The varying of times and route as far as is reasonable is a simple, but effective method. If it is also possible to vary the personnel involved occasionally, that could be useful.

There are several security firms who will undertake to carry moneys to and from the bank on your behalf. Talk to other businesses and to your bank manager, and try to get as much independent advice as possible about the various security firms who operate in your area before committing yourself; once again a talk with your local Crime Prevention Officer might prove fruitful.

PREMISES

There is a great variety of devices designed to offer security for premises, ranging from the simple idea of placing convex mirrors at strategic points within the sales or storage areas to allow vision of otherwise blind spots, to complicated networks of video cameras and monitors. The aim is to use a system which is the most appropriate to your needs and the needs of your premises.

Do not overlook the traditional alarm bell, particularly one which can be connected to your local police station. Suitable padlocks can provide adequate security for everyday situations inside and outside the building. Keeping doors open for the least possible time, particularly at goods-in when receiving deliveries is a sensible security measure.

You can still find shops which have the old-fashioned hanging bell on a spring over the shop door; at least a variation on that theme lets you know that someone has entered the premises if you have been called away from the sales area.

Ask advice of your local Crime Prevention Officer as well as your insurance company on the subject of security of premises. It could save you spending too much money – and losing a great deal of money and stock.

Advertising

Potential customers will need to know that you and your shop are there, so you need to be alert to all possibilities for advertising your business. This need not restrict itself solely to advertising material.

Insight

Find out from your local paper when they are likely to run special promotional sections like wedding fayres (they seem to like that spelling), DIY, health and beauty or gardening features. As a new shop you might be able to wangle an editorial; the advertising space will usually be cheaper, as well.

METHODS

For example, if you will be needing staff for your shop, remember that you, yourself, will be advertising your business by your appearance, manner and so forth during interviews with applicants: an excellent opportunity for creating a good business image.

Produce some suitable material – well presented – for applicants to take home: another good and subtle way of getting your name known in these critical early stages. For example, give candidates a small leaflet setting out the basic hours and working conditions, holidays and so on. Make sure the shop's name and logo are prominently displayed on the leaflet. You should also take the trouble to notify unsuccessful applicants – it is worth the price of a few stamps in goodwill.

For your more formal advertising, you will no doubt make use of the local press. Compile a Press Release feature about you and your business and talk to the advertising manager of the paper about a combined campaign – involving some straight advertising (which you pay for) and an advertising feature (which you get for free) on your business.

A less formal means of advertising, but one which could be effective for advertising the location of your premises, is a door-to-door leaflet distribution within your catchment area. Some local papers will undertake this task for you – it could be worth raising the matter when talking about advertising matters generally. Have a look at Chapter 5 to remind yourself of things to think about when producing an advertising leaflet.

Do not overlook the opportunity which the shop premises themselves provide for advertising. The actual shop front will present an image to the passing public. Suitable posters on the windows will carry particular messages, even if it is only to advertise the day of opening of your new enterprise.

TIMING

Having considered what advertising methods to use, you should also think about when to use them. Timing is significant, particularly when advertising something new, like the opening of a new shop.

Your 'Coming shortly' or 'Opening soon' advertising which could be appearing in the local press, should be timed to arouse initial interest (the AIDA formula, see Chapter 5, page 57), followed by a second wave of advertising to carry on the momentum up to the moment of opening with, perhaps, a final reminder to say 'We are now here'.

As well as the general press advertising, you might consider a leaflet distribution related specifically to the day of opening, combined with a special offer valid only for opening day.

OPENING DAY

When the great day arrives, make sure you try to get the most out of it. The use of large posters on the shop windows announcing the fact is probably a good start.

Are you considering having someone special to declare the premises open? If so, will the public come to see that person rather than buy things from your shop? Remember the value of the Press Release and of press coverage; make sure a photographer is ready to hand.

Maybe a special offer – a voucher for a free item or a reduction of a set amount handed to the first 50 customers to enter the shop – could provide useful advertising and goodwill (except from customer No. 51!).

Do not overlook the value of giving a personal welcome to those first customers as they enter the door. Putting the human touch to a business enterprise, if done well and sincerely, can only be of value to the business.

Insight

Give the last customer of the day as good a service as if they were the first customer, even though your feet are aching and you want to go home.

CHECKLIST

▶ **Siting:**
  Consider:
  - ▷ *Prime site or secondary site*
  - ▷ *Street or precinct*
  - ▷ *Size and shape*
  - ▷ *Rent and rates implications*
  - ▷ *Public transport and parking*
  - ▷ *Access for deliveries*
  - ▷ *The competition*

▶ **Image:**
  Consider:
  - ▷ *Personal service or self-service*
  - ▷ *Fixtures and fittings*
  - ▷ *Decor and lighting*
  - ▷ *Range of stock*
  - ▷ *Suppliers*
  - ▷ *Opening hours*

▶ **Stocktaking:**
  - ▷ *When will you do this?*
  - ▷ *What preparations have you made?*
  - ▷ *What are your plans for counting the stock?*

▶ **People:**
  - ▷ *How many – full- or part-time?*
  - ▷ *What hours of work?*
  - ▷ *What conditions of employment?*

▶ **Legal requirements:**
  - ▷ *Do you know the law relating to your type of business? If not, consult the Local Authority's Trading Standards Officer.*
  - ▷ *Are your premises worthy of a Fire Certificate? Consult the Fire and Rescue Service.*

▷ *Have you got third party insurance? Consult your insurance broker or insurance company.*

▶ **Money:**
  ▷ *What is your system for accepting cash, cheques, debit cards, credit cards, chip and PIN, etc.?*
  ▷ *Is it written down?*
  ▷ *Does everyone know it?*
  ▷ *What is your system for recording and banking your takings?*

▶ **Security:**
  ▷ *What do your staff know about security?*
  ▷ *How secure is your stock in the sales area, in the stockroom and at goods in?*
  ▷ *What are your security arrangements for money in the shop and money in transit to and from the bank?*
  ▷ *Are your premises fully secure at all times of the day and night?*

▶ **Advertising:**
  Consider:
  ▷ *Press*
  ▷ *Leaflet drops*
  ▷ *Posters*
  ▷ *Opening day*

13

Import and export

In this chapter:
- **Import:** *ordering from abroad; documentation; customs and transportation; payment; insurance*
- **Export:** *should you export? where to get help*

Import and export are often lumped together, as they are in the heading to this chapter, but, apart from the documentation, they are quite different. A very small firm (a sole trader) might want to import items (gifts, for example). Export is for those who have solid experience of marketing and selling their product or service on the home market before they embark on exporting. It could be part of expanding your business, but should not be undertaken from the start. This does not apply to e-commerce, of course (see Chapter 14).

Import

To import sounds more daunting than it actually is. You are merely buying from an overseas supplier instead of a home supplier, and the difference is all to do with procedures, currency and time – things which can be calculated or learnt. We deal here with the mechanics of getting the goods from overseas to your place of work – not with choosing suppliers and negotiating deals.

ORDERING FROM ABROAD

Before you place your order you should get a firm quotation from your supplier. Be very specific about what you want on the quotation; this is best done by a formal request for a quotation setting out:

- *Who you are and what your business is*
- *Who your bankers are, to help establish your creditworthiness*
- *The goods or services you want, and how they are to be packed and marked*
- *Possible questions*
- *Delivery dates and terms*
- *What insurance arrangements you intend to use.*

Once you have a firm quotation, you can place your order.

When you place an order in the UK, you know that you must be precise in what you are ordering and where it should be delivered. You also have to take into account delivery times, carriage charges and discounts.

Ordering from abroad is no different. You can order by phone, fax or email, but the order should be confirmed in writing on your headed paper. Remember to agree with your supplier:

- *Quantity, description and price*
- *Method of despatch (air, sea or land)*
- *Method of delivery (post, courier, etc.) and delivery destination (port, warehouse, etc.)*
- *Delivery times, which are likely to be longer, but not necessarily*
- *The point at which the insurance by the supplier stops and the insurance by you begins (see 'Insurance' page 197, later in this chapter)*
- *Whether the prices quoted include insurance*
- *Carriage charges*
- *Discounts*
- *Method of payment.*

If you are doing regular business with a supplier, it may be beneficial to set up a trading agreement and account.

When considering quotations and pricing, take into account that currency values fluctuate, so you need to be sure which currency you are dealing in and in which currency the price is fixed. For large orders, buyers can secure the price well in advance of delivery by taking a 'position' or 'option' on the currency value with the bank. This needs some knowledge and experience of currency markets and values.

In EU countries, if you are using suppliers and you are VAT registered, you may not have to pay VAT on the goods you purchase. In any case if you pay VAT, it will be at the UK rate, not at the rate of the supplying country.

Insight

You may choose to collect your supplies yourself and ship them across the Channel in your own vehicle. It might be wise to arrive at the port in your van at a busy time, not early in the morning, when HM Revenue & Customs Officers are looking for something to do.

DOCUMENTATION

Advice Note	On receipt of your order, the supplier should confirm to you all the details mentioned above, including date of expected despatch and length of delivery time
Bill of Lading	This is the receipt given by a ship's master to the supplier of goods, stating in detail the goods loaded on board the ship. The Bill of Lading is an important part of the papers which travel with goods being imported or exported
Air Waybill	This is a sort of aviation Bill of Lading. It is a contract of carriage when goods are sent by air, and acts as a receipt for the goods. It is made out by the airline
Delivery Note	A detailed description, from the supplier, of the actual goods in that delivery
Carriage Note	Details, from a transport company, of the number of crates, boxes or pallets
Pro Forma Invoice	You will also receive a Pro Forma Invoice, probably stating the preferred method of payment

These are the most common items of documentation. For details of customs and other documents, seek advice from your clearing agent.

CUSTOMS AND TRANSPORTATION

If you are intending to import fairly large quantities of goods, it could be wise, to start with, to use a clearing agent, who will deal with all the customs and transport side of it for you. Seek advice from your local Chamber of Commerce.

> **Insight**
>
> Don't think you can get away with going on a booze cruise and bringing home large quantities of alcohol and cigarettes for re-sale! These items are for personal use only, and HM Revenue & Customs have many different methods of checking the contents of your vehicle.

If you are importing on a very small or limited basis, the Post Office is an excellent transporter of goods. Your supplier will complete all the customs documentation necessary. If the order is a sample, and not for onward sale by you, ask the supplier to mark the goods 'Sample only – of no commercial value'. This should mean that you do not have to pay customs duty.

You will probably have to collect your packages from the sorting office, and pay any VAT and duty due at that point. You will probably have to pay a Post Office clearance fee. Keep the Post Office label on the package, as this will constitute your VAT receipt for book-keeping purposes.

PAYMENT

Bear in mind that some overseas suppliers may require payment up front because you have little or no trading history. They will usually require this to be done through a Bank Transfer, which will incur bank charges for you. Some suppliers will not accept orders below a minimum amount.

You may also be asked for trade references, which can be difficult for new enterprises.

As in the UK, damaged items must be reported immediately to the supplier, who will usually issue a Credit Note against subsequent orders.

The main methods of payment are:

Cash
Sent by registered post. This is popular among less developed countries for small orders.

Via the bank
The most normal way of paying your suppliers is by Bank Transfer. Send a letter of authorization to your bank detailing account numbers and accounts.

Via the Post Office
An International Payment Coupon (rather like a Postal Order) can be bought at the Post Office and sent by post to the supplier. It is suitable for small amounts.

INSURANCE

You need to be sure that your goods are insured until they reach your doorstep. These are the most common terms used when despatching goods:

FOB (Free on Board)	The price quoted includes everything until the goods are loaded onto the ship or plane. This does not include insurance
CIF (Cost Insurance Freight)	Means that everything is covered, including insurance, up to delivery at your warehouse except the cost of transport from the port or airport in the UK. You will have to arrange and pay for the cost of this transport, but the goods remain insured

C&F	Means that the goods are not insured so
(Cost and Freight)	you will have to make your own insurance
	arrangements

As you can see, it is important that you are clear about the terms under which your goods will be supplied, so make sure they appear on the quotation you have requested.

Importing small quantities of goods is quite easy, particularly if you use the postal services. Importing large quantities is obviously more complicated. Seek all the advice you can before you start. Importing from EU countries should be a simpler matter.

Export

There are many rewards to be gained from a sound export business, but you should not embark on this until you are sure you have a viable and solid business base in the UK.

When exporting, you will need to consider all the aspects of selling that you have been carrying on, but at a distance and in a market which you probably do not know. Think of carrying out market research, marketing, selling, transporting, getting paid and all the other aspects of your business in another country, and you will see that exporting is not for the beginner. Having said that, your product or service might be a very marketable commodity abroad.

You will need help to set about exporting your product, so this chapter will confine itself to giving you guidance on where to look for that help.

UK Trade &	This is a government organization whose
Investment	aim is to help UK firms make a success of
	their exporting business. Visit their website
	(www.tradeinvest. gov.uk) for a wealth of
	information

Institute of Export	An institute specializing in the export business, with good experience of exporting for small businesses. Visit their website at www.export.org.uk
SITPRO	Simplifying International Trade tries to simplify procedures and paperwork and generally help the efficiency of export and payment. Visit their website at www.sitpro.org.uk
Embassies	The embassy of the country to which you are intending to export can give excellent advice on local distributors, customs, banking arrangements, etc.

CHECKLIST

▶ **Import:**

Use this checklist for each order you place:

▷ *Have you got a firm quotation?*
▷ *Does the quotation cover all details?*
▷ *Has all the documentation been completed?*
▷ *How will you handle customs?*
▷ *How will you get the goods to your doorstep?*
▷ *Which method of payment will you use?*
▷ *Are your goods properly insured?*

▶ **Export:**

▷ *Are you ready to export yet?*
▷ *If the answer is 'Yes', seek help and advice from the organizations mentioned in this chapter.*

14

e-commerce

In this chapter:

- *Know your customers*
- *Getting started*
- *Open an eBay shop*
- *Your own website: choose your website name; register your website name; design your website*
- *Photographs*
- *Despatch*
- *Copyright*
- *Marketing*
- *Running costs*
- *Funding*

You may decide to sell your products on-line from the start, or choose to expand your business into selling on-line, which means potentially selling worldwide. The steps you need to take are much the same as for selling products face-to-face, but the detail within those steps will vary.

Insight

Chester House Productions doesn't sell on-line. After all, we are live theatre. But we do use our website to give information and let our customers know who our past and future bookings are for, so they get some idea of whether our products (theatre productions) will meet their needs.

Know your customers

Chapter 1 asks questions about your product, your customers and your own ability to sell, and suggests you do a pilot scheme, if possible. When selling face-to-face you get to know who your customers are, but on-line you have no idea who they will be or where they will live.

So do a little market research and look at websites which sell products similar to yours. You can usually tell the sort of customer who would buy those products by looking at the product design, the cost and the website design itself. You will also get some idea of what other people charge, whether they include postage and packing and how easy it is to order and pay for their products.

Make notes of what you like about their website and their products and what you don't like. Decide whether your products will have a good chance of selling well in that particular market. (What are your USPs – unique selling points?) Then, if you are totally new to e-commerce, run a pilot scheme, perhaps starting on eBay.

Getting started

You need to get used to e-commerce in a small way to start with. You may well already have bought on-line, so you know what it is like from the customer's point of view, but selling on-line 'feels' quite different. A good place to start on a personal level before you start selling commercially is eBay.

Buy something on eBay first, any small item you need, so you can begin to find your way round the site. Remember eBay is an auction site, so the starting price is likely to be quite low – a 'come and buy me' price. Once you have got used to buying, you can start selling through eBay, again in a small way, perhaps something personal you don't mind getting rid of at a fairly low cost.

You will need a reasonable photograph of what you want to sell and a good description of the item. eBay has good advice and will help you through this process, for example how your 'customer' is to pay for your item (or items) and how you will deliver it.

Once you are familiar with the process of buying and selling on-line, you can begin to sell a few of your own products, perhaps through the eBay shop, before embarking on your own website. You need to have sold enough items personally to earn a feedback score of 10 or more before you can open your eBay shop.

Open an eBay shop

Before you set up your own website, you could try opening an eBay shop. There are various types of shop; you will probably want to start with a Basic Shop, aimed at sellers just starting out. Do follow the instructions and advice given on eBay, which are very helpful.

You are not allowed to buy or make items for resale as a business while pretending to be a private seller. You will have to register your business and create a seller's account to verify your identity and set up arrangements for paying your seller's fee. Yes, you have to pay a fee – eBay is a business too.

On the other hand, you might decide to go straight in to designing and selling through your own website.

Insight

One of our local charities, for people with a disability, will take on the task of selling a personal item on eBay on our behalf: we supply the photo and description, and the item is added to the eBay auction. Any profit is divided between the charity and us. Of course, this doesn't help us explore undertaking e-commerce for our business.

Your own website

CHOOSE YOUR WEBSITE NAME

If you are already in business and have decided to expand into
e-commerce, you will already have a business name. You will need
to be sure that the name you choose says something about your
business. 'Carousel Creations', for example, could be about anything,
but 'Carousel Cottage Crafts' gives a far better idea of what the
business is about and what you are likely to be offering for sale.

REGISTER YOUR WEBSITE NAME

Check whether your business name is available on '.co.uk' and
'.com'. Remember, '.co.uk' caters for the UK market, while '.com'
reaches the market worldwide, especially the USA. Also useful is
'.eu' if your business is likely to focus on Europe.

When you try to register your name, your ISP (Internet Service
Provider) will quickly let you know whether your chosen name is
available or not. You might have to tweak it a little to register it as
a domain name. Once registered, your name will be accessible to
anyone with an internet connection.

DESIGN YOUR WEBSITE

A good design is just so important it's worth employing a
professional to do this for you, unless you know you are good
at doing that sort of thing yourself. If you are computer literate
enough to design your own, you could use a free e-commerce
package like Zen Cart to get you started.

Alternatively, you could use a hosted service through your ISP.
A hosted service provides a complete on-line service, including
buying a domain name, setting up and managing an on-line shop
and making payment arrangements. You would simply enter your
products, which itself takes a lot of time. One drawback is that the

range of e-commerce options can be quite narrow, and you will have no control over expanding them. However, it might be a good way of doing a pilot scheme to see if your products really sell.

Perhaps you are ready to sell through your own website, so this is what you will need to do. Having chosen and registered your domain name, design your web pages to include:

A 'Home' page

This will include your company name and logo and be designed in your company colours, if you have any. Write a couple of introductory paragraphs describing your products and what makes them different. Include your USPs, which the search engines will pick up. Your Home page introduces your products to the world.

Insight

A strapline, or sort of sub-title, is useful. Our Chester House Productions strapline is 'Social history through theatre', which gives a good idea of what we actually do. Search engines will pick up the key words 'productions', 'social history' and 'theatre'. Our Home page also refers to 'professional' and 'speakers', which is what our customers are searching for.

A page for each category of product

This is where your products are described in detail, together with good photographs (see *Photographs* later in this chapter). You need to put all the information a customer would want to know, such as size, colour(s), catalogue number (if any), model etc., together with the price per item.

Insight

Check your product descriptions for spelling, grammar and punctuation. Preferably get someone else to check this. One small example: if you see an item is 'complimentary' (with an 'i') it means that it's free; if you say it's 'complementary' (with an 'e') it means it's in addition to, and will complement another of your items. Just one wrong spelling could cost you money!

This takes ages to do well. You have to take the photos, making sure they are all the same size, with a background which suits the colour of your web page and write the descriptions, checking that all the details are accurate. You might, for example, need to include the weight of an item, which means you must weigh it and give the weight in kilos and/or grams or pounds and ounces. Remember to give sizes in metric and imperial, too.

A page for ordering and payment, linked to your product pages
Make the ordering process as simple as possible so that customers can easily add items to their 'basket'. Oh, and do you want the icon of a basket, or would a shopping trolley be more appropriate?

One of the best methods of payment is Paypal, as you will have discovered if you have been shopping or selling on eBay. This is a secure method of conducting financial transactions and retains the confidentiality of your customer's bank account or credit card. Payment is cleared straight away, so you can quickly get the goods packed up and sent off. It also sends an automatic acknowledgement to your customer. Don't accept cash, except from very close friends and family.

Will you charge for postage and packing? It is usually simpler to make this free in the UK, but to charge to send products overseas. You will have to ask your customers to ring (or email) to find out what the charges are, so they can add it to their payment. Make sure your phone number and email address are prominently displayed on this page as well as on your 'Contact us' page.

A terms and conditions page
This need not be too long and daunting, but it should detail your company policies, for example: payment must be received before items are despatched; postage and packing are free in the UK; the cost of items returned within a certain time will be refunded. Look at your competitors' websites to see what their terms and conditions are.

An 'About us' page

This is your chance to describe your company and what it does. Photographs of your premises, your people and even the company cat add a human touch to your business. Customers also like to know a little about the history of your company, but don't make it too long or dense.

A 'Contact us' page

Here you can give all the contact details you want your customers to know, including an email link which will come through directly to you. Be careful not to reveal confidential details, your bank name for example. This is common sense, but it is surprising what people will, unintentionally, give away.

As you can see, this part of setting up your e-commerce business is time-consuming. So plan in enough time to get all this done, particularly if you are seeking funding, and include the timing in your business plan.

Photographs

Websites cry out for good photographs and/or moving images. You, or your website designer, can create a 'flash banner' at the top of your 'Home' page and other pages, which contains photos of your main products to catch a customer's eye. The photos 'flash' on and off at given intervals, so you can have several photos showing in turn.

Insight

A digital camera, with flash, will be all you need to start with. Make sure the photograph is big enough for your potential buyer to see detail and put all the necessary information in your description. Ask yourself, 'If I were a buyer, what would I need to know?'

You can certainly learn good photography skills, given time, if you do not possess these already. To start with, your own digital camera, with flash, will probably be sufficient.

Use a plain background and some good, directional lighting, if you can, to pick up highlights on your products and bring them to life. On your desktop or laptop manipulate or refine/crop your photos so they are all the same size with the same background. You can airbrush out an unwanted bit of background, if necessary. You can probably, at the early stages, make do with a good word processing package (Word) for your product descriptions and an image manipulation program for your photos (Photoshop).

Shoot the items from different angles, if appropriate, to show off all your products' good points. If possible design the website so your customers can click on a photo to enlarge it. The more idea they have of what a product actually looks like, with true colours, the better.

Despatch

Once you have received payment, pack and despatch the goods as soon as you can. People who shop on the web expect prompt delivery. Use second class post for the UK and airmail for all other destinations for small items. Make friends with your local Post Office, who will advise you on what you can and cannot send by post. See Chapter 13 on import and export about despatching goods overseas.

Pack and wrap all your items securely; you don't want to lose business because of items damaged in transit. Get your friends and family to let you have their spare bubble wrap or other packing materials, which they will almost certainly have if they have been shopping on-line. For very precious and breakable items, you can use specialist services who will charge for their expertise. Do check the insurance arrangements.

Include a Despatch Note giving details of the order, and any items 'to follow'. Be sure to do this if you are doing personal selling on eBay, because you are not allowed to use your trading name. You can use this opportunity to refer your customers to your website.

Copyright

If you are designing and making your own products, the copyright or intellectual property rights will lie with you. However, if you incorporate into your design someone else's ideas or products, you might be breaching their copyright. A design based on a photo you have taken yourself is fine, but the copyright for a design based on, perhaps, a photo in a magazine will not be entirely yours.

If you are ever accused of breaching someone's copyright (and this includes their domain name), do three things: ask for details of the alleged breach, make no comment and contact your lawyer. Copyright, particularly on the internet, is a minefield.

Marketing

Once your website is up and running, you need to let people know it exists. Make sure you get good key words about your product (e.g. individually-designed, or bespoke, or natural) in your strap line and in your introductory paragraphs on your 'Home' page, so that search engines can find you.

Use your personal contacts: friends, family, networking clubs, etc. Give out flyers, or even small brochures, with the details of your exciting new website and e-commerce business. They will help spread the word.

Include on your website feedback and testimonials from your customers. Ask their permission first. Look after these customers well, so they give you good scores on their buying experience.

Insight

For each of our 'products', the web page includes 'What audience members have said'. These are genuine. We wouldn't make them up!

Running costs

As with any other form of business, you will have bills to pay, invoices to raise and payments to record. Programs such as eBay and Zen Cart will help you there, but you must keep all your records straight.

Your expenditure is likely to include normal overheads (lighting, heating, etc.) packing materials, raw materials, possibly storage space rental. You will also have to pay for:

▶ *your website designer, if you do not do this yourself*
▶ *website maintenance, likewise*
▶ *the registration of your domain name and its annual renewal*
▶ *eBay listings, if you use these*
▶ *fees for managing receipts through PayPal, if you use this*
▶ *postage*

Insight

If your customers pay through PayPal the payment is cleared straight away. If they send a cheque, by the time it is received, banked and cleared, ten or more days may have passed. Don't despatch items until full payment has been received.

The costs of buying a desktop, laptop or digital camera are treated as capital costs, and may not be claimed for tax purposes.

Insight

You will probably be able to find a one-day course on e-commerce for beginners in your locality. Try the local authority, Business Link or your local college.

Funding

As you can see, your start-up costs could be quite considerable, so you may need some funding to get you off the ground. Many local authorities are quite keen to encourage small businesses, including e-commerce, so you could start your quest for funds there.

The Department for Work and Pensions at present offers six-month free support in the form of New Deal. They appoint a business adviser who will meet you regularly and help you plan and set deadlines. New Deal also pays your National Insurance for six months and can enrol you on various courses. Governments often change their support facilities, and New Deal may no longer exist, but it is worth looking up the DWP website to see what is on offer.

For advice on approaching a bank or building society, or special funding arrangements if you are under 25 or over 50, see Chapter 2.

Setting up your e-commerce business can be a lengthy and rather scary process, but it can be quite thrilling when orders start coming in from all over the world. Check that you have done everything you need to do to get your e-commerce business soundly established.

CHECKLIST

Have you...

▶ *Checked your competitors?*

▶ *Created your company name and logo?*

▶ *Registered your domain name?*

▶ *Decided who is to design and maintain your website?*

▶ *Written the text for all your descriptive website pages?*

▶ *Compiled your ordering and payments page?*

▶ *Taken and refined your photographs?*

▶ *Written your terms and conditions and your returns policy?*

▶ *Asked someone else to proofread it all?*

▶ *Checked for any copyright problems?*

▶ *Marketed your new e-commerce on-line and locally?*

15

Running a home and
a business

In this chapter:
- *Planning ahead*
- *Children and other dependants*
- *Your health*
- *Your business image*
- *Money*

Starting your own business is hard work, and takes a lot of
time and energy. Unless the domestic side of your life is well
organized, you will find it very difficult to give the business
the concentration it needs. If you get to work worrying about
the gardening or the ironing which did not get done, you will
find it difficult to give your whole attention to your business
matters. You need to be either the sort of person who does
not mind living in chaos at home – and whose family does not
mind living in chaos either – or the sort of person who is well
organized.

We all have our own way of organizing our domestic life, so this
chapter does not say that you should or should not do certain
things. It tries to give you some ideas which will help you to
organize yourself and your family to include the extra business
dimension.

If you are working as a partnership, as we do, life can be
difficult if one of you is organized and the other one isn't.
We are both very organized people, so the administration
side of our business runs smoothly. We are also organized
domestically, but are fortunate enough to have a house with
plenty of storage space.

Planning ahead

No matter how much other people in the household help, it is still
very important to plan the routine, which includes either shopping
or, at the very least, making a shopping list.

If you have been used to shopping frequently – perhaps a little every
day or so – you will need to think about shopping less often, so that
it is not so time-consuming. If you run a freezer efficiently, you do
not need to shop more often than once a week, providing you plan
ahead. Some people do a 'bake-in' for the whole week ahead as well.

It is useful to keep a note in your diary of what everyone else is
doing, as well as your own business engagements, and a family
diary or wall chart is a great help. If you can persuade members of
the household to declare what they are going to be doing at least
a week ahead, and put it down in the family diary, it helps you to
plan who needs to eat what, and when. Try not to keep too many
diaries (one personal and one family should be enough) or you will
find it difficult to keep them up to date.

You will also need to plan ahead for such things as:

▶ *children's activities*
▶ *business dinners*
▶ *family holidays and breaks*
▶ *visits to the vet (if you have pets)*
▶ *visits from service engineers, etc.*

- *clothes shopping*
- *social and leisure activities.*

It may sound a bit regimented if you are not used to planning your life in this way, but if you like to live an organized sort of life, you will find that careful planning is essential to your peace of mind and the success of your business. It also gives the family a sense of security, although you have to guard against a lack of flexibility: always having smoked mackerel salad on a Friday starts as a joke, but can finally become an irritant.

DIVISION OF LABOUR

If you are to run your business successfully, you really do need the support of the people at home, not just occasionally, but all the time. It is illogical for people to sit around waiting for you to get home to get the evening meal: perhaps a 'first in starts the meal' routine would work in your household.

Insight

Love is… having the dinner ready when the other one gets home and greeting him or her with a glass of something cool and refreshing.

Each family will have its own way of sorting out who does what, but it is important that everyone, including the smallest of the children, does something on a regular basis. Three-year-olds can tidy their toys away; five-year-olds can dust; ten-year-olds can help prepare vegetables; fourteen-year-olds can cope with washing, ironing and cooking. Everyone can help with the washing up and the cleaning. Discuss these things with the family, and see who can do what, and how they can best fit it in with their own timetable. Obviously only adults can drive cars, but almost everyone can push a hoover around.

In some households the chores seem to fall naturally into traditional male and female jobs; in others, who does what is by preference. Women often find that only they are prepared to clean the lavatory and the bath. You can encourage everyone in the family to look after their personal belongings, which means both male and female cleaning their shoes and doing their mending – again there is no logical reason why they should not.

In a busy household the garden often gets neglected. If you are a tidy person, this will niggle away at the back of your mind, particularly if you care what the neighbours say – and many people do. It is helpful to have a garden which is easy to cope with, and which other family members do not mind working in. Go for easily-kept lawns and shrubs, or patios. Plenty of ground cover keeps the weeds at bay. No garden will look reasonable if left totally unattended – even if your garden is a window box, the plants still need watering – but you can make it easier for yourself and other members of the household if you plan the garden carefully and agree with the others on who will do what. Gardening can be a very good way of getting away from the business for a while, and you will need to do that from time to time.

USING HELP

Some people manage to do everything superbly well: they run a business, a house and a social life, and have really good relationships with people at home and at work, and you wonder how they do it.

One of the secrets often is that they use all the help they can get, both human and mechanical. Reliable help with the cleaning, washing, ironing and mending is not easy to find, but if you can find someone at least to do the heavy cleaning, it is well worth the expense. You need not feel guilty or inadequate because you are paying someone else to do what perhaps you consider is your responsibility. You are earning money elsewhere, and you cannot do everything yourself; employing someone to help in the home or the garden benefits you and the person you are employing to do the job. It may take time to find the right person, but it is worth persevering. Using help is a strength, not a weakness.

216

You should also use all the mechanical help you can get, such as a really efficient washing machine and dryer, a dishwasher, a microwave, if you like that method of cooking. Use appliances which make your life, and that of everyone else in the household, easier. This might mean updating your appliances more frequently than you are used to doing. It is normally worth the money and the effort.

TIME AND PEOPLE

Your business will find it more difficult to thrive if your domestic background is unstable. This means making time to be with your home partner and the children, if you have any. You might have to work some evenings and weekends, but if you make it every evening and weekend, undercurrents of dissatisfaction are likely to start up at home, and you will lose the goodwill and support of the people you need most.

Children need a stable home base, and they need to know that their parents have the time and the interest to care about their activities and their worries. This is common sense, of course, but it is amazing how easy it is to get caught up in the excitement and freedom of doing your own thing, and to forget, very gradually, how much you are needed and wanted at home. It is a fine balance to strike, but if sensitively handled need not mean that either home or business has to suffer.

Children and other dependants

You might be the type of person who feels guilty at letting other people look after the children or other dependants – an elderly relative, perhaps. Very few people – especially women – escape this sense of guilt at some time or other, particularly when they leave a new baby in the care of others for the first time. Other members of the family, perhaps your own parents, can often make you feel guilty as well, sometimes quite deliberately.

One way of coping with this is to acknowledge the sense of guilt, and then do everything that you can to make sure that your children and other dependants are well cared for when you are not with them. This section will concentrate on caring for children. Make sure you have done all the necessary child protection checks.

NANNIES

Nannies look after children in your own home. This can be as a live-in nanny, a daily nanny, or one who lives in during the week and goes home at the weekends.

Some nannies have been to top-class training establishments, and are fully qualified in all aspects of child care. The training is thorough, and expensive. A qualified nanny will be seeking a well-paid position, often as a live-in nanny, with excellent domestic facilities, working conditions and hours. These are often the nannies who answer advertisements in *The Lady*, which seems to be the leading 'top nanny' recruitment medium, if one can put it that way. These nannies will have excellent references, and can be relied upon to do a thoroughly competent and reliable job, combined with real care for the children, in a suitable household.

If you are looking for a less highly qualified nanny, who perhaps will look after your children on a daily basis, and sometimes on a job-share basis (some hours or days with you, some with another family), look in local nanny agencies, Job Centres and advertisements in the local paper. You can advertise in the local paper yourself, of course.

Agencies do not necessarily 'screen' the applicants for your particular job – some do and some do not. You usually have to pay a registration fee as an employer and the agency will send you prospective nannies for you to interview. You need to find out from the agency what you are paying for – it might be just the introduction, or the agency might do a certain amount of selection on your behalf. They will need to know how much you are prepared to pay (usually by the hour); an agency or a Job Centre can advise you on this.

What are you looking for in a nanny? Obviously someone who likes and can deal with children. When you interview a prospective nanny, make sure it is at a time when your children are around and awake. Let the nanny play with them or hold them, and watch the reactions of the nanny and the children.

It is also important that the nanny's personality is compatible with yours. If you have a fairly strong personality (and you have to be able to acknowledge this), a nanny with an equally forceful outlook on life could cause problems. On the other hand, you do not want anyone who is not capable of following instructions and taking decisions when necessary. There can be clashes of culture as well as personality; young nannies sometimes move from one part of the country to another, or from one country to another, and their diet and background could be quite different from yours and what you want for your children. This need not be a problem if you are clear about what you want, and if you are both prepared to be understanding and a little flexible. It is something to consider when engaging a nanny to look after your children.

A nanny will expect to do everything connected with the children, according to the hours of work agreed. At the start you will need to make lists of the children's routines, roughly what you would like them to eat for their meals, what you want them to wear, and so on. A nanny will not expect to do the housework, except where it is directly connected with the children – their clothes, their meals. Unless you have fairly well-delineated areas of work, there can be conflict between a nanny and, say, the person who does the cleaning in the house: the one could resent what the other does and does not do. Incidentally, cleaning ladies often get paid rather more than nannies.

MOTHER'S OR FATHER'S HELP

A Mother's or Father's Help is someone (usually a woman) who is prepared to do a bit of everything – looking after the children and some domestic work. These women are not often professionally qualified, but are quite capable of looking after children and doing some of the domestic chores, such as light cleaning, washing and ironing. They would expect to be paid more than just a nanny or just a cleaner, but could be less expensive than employing both.

You will find Mother's or Father's Helps through agencies, Job Centres and advertisements in the local press. You both (employer and employed) need to be clear about what you expect, what the job entails and what the payment is going to be. A Mother's or Father's Help is also someone who is going to look after your children, so you need to be just as careful about selection as if you were employing a nanny.

AU PAIRS

These are (usually) young women from abroad whose main aim is to live in England for a while to improve their English. They will normally want to live in with the family, so need reasonable living accommodation and time off. They will probably be happy to do light housework as well as look after the children.

Because an au pair is usually a young person, you will have a certain amount of responsibility for her welfare in this country, and you will probably be required to allow her specific time off to pursue her English studies.

It is helpful to employ au pairs through agencies who specialize in this area of work, because they can advise you on your responsibilities as well as what you can expect from an au pair. An au pair will not expect to be paid a great deal of money, but she will expect to live and be treated as part of the family.

CHILDMINDERS

If your business allows you to work regular hours and you can be sure to deliver and collect your children, a registered childminder can be a good way of making sure your children are well cared for. Childminders often have children of their own at home, and are happy to add to their family on a regular basis and look after other people's children as well as their own.

Childminders have to be registered with the local authority because their facilities, safety and competence are monitored. Lists of registered childminders can be obtained from the Social Services department of your Local Authority. Many childminders are prepared to look after your children for long hours, or for odd hours, provided it is on a regular basis.

ILLNESS AND HOLIDAYS

It is when your children are ill that you are likely to feel most torn between your business and your family. Perhaps you have an important client to meet, and a phone call comes through that your child is ill. What do you do? Perhaps your instincts are to rush home and let the client know that the meeting will have to be postponed. On the other hand, you are in business, and if you have not got a business partner who can cover for you, perhaps your domestic partner, or another member of the family, can cope with the immediate problem, and you can take it from there. Make all necessary arrangements, and try to put the illness out of your mind until you have completed your business, unless of course it is very serious. Then you can drop everything else and give your child all your attention.

Holidays are another matter and can be planned for. Some local authorities provide facilities for looking after children too young to be left on their own during the school holidays and half terms. One of the benefits of being self-employed is that you can sometimes arrange your workload round school holidays, depending on the nature of the business and the people with whom you work.

If you have to leave young teenagers on their own during the day, they sometimes find it acceptable for you to leave, every morning, a plan of action for the day, which can include jobs to do and, perhaps, outings or activities that you have pre-arranged or for which you have bought a ticket. It takes quite a lot of thought and organization on your part, but can be useful for only children, or children whose friends have all decided to be away at the same time.

Holidays do not just take care of themselves. Again it helps to plan fairly carefully, but allow some flexibility.

OTHER DEPENDANTS

It depends whether other people who are dependent on you are living in your house or on their own. In either case, if they have been used to having you around, it is going to be difficult for both parties to accept that some of your time is going to be allocated elsewhere. You may face accusations that you are unfeeling and ambitious, which again, will make you feel guilty.

As with children, provided you have made every provision possible for the care and welfare of dependent relatives (home helps, local shopping services, meals on wheels), there is no reason why you should not go about your business with a clear mind. Enlist the help of other members of your family, including your own children and your domestic partner, and remember your own brothers and sisters.

Involve dependants in the decisions which have to be made, and share with them as far as possible the excitement – and the worries – of running your own business. It could add an extra dimension to their lives.

Your health

When you are self-employed you cannot afford to be ill, and you usually have not got the time to be ill. Certainly a busy life and being really interested in what you are doing makes you less inclined to have or notice minor ailments.

As far as major illnesses are concerned, you need to do all you can to prevent these. Your lifestyle and regular medical checkups will make sure you are healthy and fit to maintain the energy and stamina which you will certainly need.

YOUR LIFESTYLE

When you are very busy, you are tempted not to eat properly. Stress and digestive disorders can build up if you never have breakfast, do not stop for lunch, rush home and get the evening meal and then eat it in a hurry. If you can discipline yourself to have a definite break for lunch, even if it is only a short one, your productivity will remain high in the afternoon.

Sometimes you can get caught up in a lot of business lunches; too many of those can ruin your figure as well as your digestion. However, it is acceptable to be seen not to eat too much at lunchtime and not to drink too much. In fact, women have an advantage here, because they do not have to project a macho image. You can easily drift into high alcohol consumption, but fortunately it is now quite all right to be seen not to drink if you are driving, or to have mineral water with your lunch or dinner wine.

It goes without saying, and is common sense, that a well-balanced diet is what you need to keep healthy. The problem is that you can get so busy trying to run at least two lives at once that you ignore this aspect of your lifestyle, and eat and drink too much or too little.

It is not easy to fit in regular exercise, because often you cannot stick to a very strict timetable. But if you can swim, walk, do keep fit, play tennis or squash or do something in the way of exercise on a regular basis, it will certainly help to keep your body trim and of course your clothes will look better on you. At the very least, walk up stairs instead of taking lifts, do not ride where you can walk and try to get a little exercise in every day.

Some people seem to survive on very little sleep, and some people need a lot. Whatever your necessary quota, try to make sure that you get it. If someone is ill, you cannot, perhaps, help staying up all night, but it does not do you any good to lie awake worrying – the problem will not be solved, and your body and mind will not be refreshed. Try to finish all you have to do before you go to bed, and be determined to leave everything else until the next day. Some people can catnap during the day, and find this refreshing; if you are that type of person, it can be better to stop off at a motorway service station for 15 minutes and have a sleep, rather than arrive feeling worn out. If you do decide to sleep in your car, remember to shut all windows and lock all doors for safety's sake, and park in the middle of the car park rather than in a quiet corner.

If you are able to fit it in, it is a good idea to spend some time each week doing something which has nothing to do with work, and nothing to do with home. Regular exercise can be one such activity, but joining a group to share interests or learn something new can be equally relaxing and therapeutic. You need a little time for yourself.

PREVENTIVE MEDICINE

If you are self-employed you cannot claim sickness benefit from an employer or from the state. Some people take out insurance cover for lost earnings if they are sick, as well as covering the cost of treatment to enable them to get back to work as quickly as possible.

Another form of insurance is to have a full, regular medical checkup, probably annually. These are given at Well Woman, or Well Man Clinics, which are sometimes available on the National Health, or privately. A regular checkup means that any illness can be detected at an early stage, and the cure is often swift and complete – less time away from your business. Women should take advantage of breast screening and cervical smear testing, particularly if they are in the high-risk age groups.

As well as detecting the early signs of disease, a doctor giving you regular checkups can also advise you on your general health. It is obvious to you if you are putting on or losing too much weight, but high blood pressure or a high cholesterol level is not obvious. These are checked in a full medical, and your doctor will advise you on diet and exercise.

Addiction to smoking or drugs of any sort, including tranquillizers, will damage your health. If you know you take too many pills, or cannot stop smoking, seek help. You cannot afford to let such things drain away your energies. If as a woman you know you suffer from PMT or 'disabling' periods, go to your doctor. There are often things which can be done to alleviate discomfort, and you might as well take the trouble to sort these things out, rather than put up with it every month.

Your health is very precious, and you need to be in good health to run a business successfully. Look after it.

Insight

We have throughout the years had regular checkups. We are, fortunately, generally very healthy. At one checkup, apologizing to the doctor for being rather boring, the reply came back, 'Never be interesting to your doctor.' It's a good maxim!

Your business image

You are in business, and need to look, sound and appear businesslike. This means that your whole image should reflect you and the type of business you run. It does not mean that women have to give up their femininity, but nor should they exploit it.

YOUR APPEARANCE

Try to choose a style of dress and hairstyle which suits you and the image you want to project. This does not necessarily mean that you need to keep up with the latest fashion detail, unless you are in that type of business yourself. It does mean that you need to keep your wardrobe reasonably up to date in both style and colour.

It can be a good idea to buy several items which you can mix and match, having chosen your colour scheme for the season or the year. There are many businesses who can advise you on the sort of style and colouring which is the best for you and your particular image. If you are the sort of person who finds it difficult to decide on what is best for you, a visit to that type of establishment could be a worthwhile investment. You can find their advertisements in professional and business magazines and publications, and they usually cater for both men and women.

If your wardrobe has been geared to a home environment, you will need to take time to plan and build up a business wardrobe gradually. Your hair needs to be easy to look after, and yet look smart and stylish, without being way out. For a woman, a style which can be washed frequently and dried with ease is a great asset – and so is an efficient hairdryer.

Insight

People doing back-stage work always dress in black, so when we arrive at a venue and do the 'get-in', we both wear black, and sweatshirts with 'Chester House Productions' printed on them. This means we are easily identifiable to our customers. Once we have got everything set up, we can turn our attention to costumes and makeup. Then we reverse the process for the 'get-out'.

Again, for a woman, it is important to be strict about not driving in business shoes – nothing ruins the heels more quickly. It is worth having a pair of driving shoes which you keep in the car and which you can slip on and off easily. Keep a spare pair of knee-highs or stockings in your briefcase.

Bags and briefcases say a lot about you. If your bag or briefcase is in a muddle, you will project a muddly image. A slim briefcase, containing only the papers you need for that day, shows an orderly mind, and therefore an orderly way of doing business. If your bag or briefcase is of good quality it will last longer and project a quality image of you. Buy as good as you can afford. It does not enhance your image to arrive with an overflowing, cheap bag and a plastic carrier bag!

Your car is part of your image too. It does not matter if it is small and elderly, provided it is well cared for and clean. A car full of children's bits and pieces is not a good idea; try to leave those at home.

YOUR SOCIAL SKILLS

When greeting anyone for the first time, shake hands, firmly; do the same when saying goodbye. It helps to break down the initial barrier between you and to end a meeting on a friendly note. Most meetings, whether they are large, formal meetings or small, informal ones usually start off with some smalltalk between you and your neighbour. Stick to neutral topics like the weather, the journey or the car park. People do not want to talk, at that stage, about burning issues of the day, or about domestic topics. However, it is useful to keep up to date with what is going on in current affairs, the business world and/or sport, so that you can talk with a reasonable amount of knowledge about these things, if the occasion arises.

Accept offers of tea, coffee or other refreshments, and be definite about how you like it. Changing your mind about such apparently trivial matters at the start of a business meeting is not a good beginning.

Some men still regard businesswomen with suspicion. They can feel superior, or threatened, or both. If you are a woman in business treat men with quiet confidence, showing that you know your business but have no wish to be over-friendly, and you should not have any problems. Some men are quite happy to do business with women, but still like to treat them as women in such matters as opening doors, carrying heavy loads and so on. Do not expect men to do this, but if they wish to do so, accept graciously. It makes them feel good and will not diminish your standing in any way.

Remember that some decisions are made in the Gents or the Ladies; be aware of several men or women disappearing at the same time and returning with a united front. If you are aware of such things, you can counteract them if necessary.

It is worthwhile learning about food and wines, if you do not already know these things, so that you can handle situations in bars and restaurants with confidence and ease. You do not have to be over-assertive, but you can make your position known with calm authority, and you should do so.

As a person starting out in business you need to earn the respect of other business people in all sorts of situations.

Money

KEEP YOUR BUSINESS MONEY SEPARATE

It is important to keep your business and domestic money separate. Since 1990 women have been separately taxed and assessed anyway, and this will include unearned income – building society interest and so on. But keeping the money separate goes much further than that.

> **Insight**
> We each have our personal bank account, as well as our business account, and are careful to pay credit card bills from the right account. Sometimes this can mean sending three cheques! We take it in turns to top up the housekeeping cash.

If you start mixing up the money you use for housekeeping with your business money, particularly if part or all of that is supplied by your domestic partner, your book-keeping will get in a hopeless muddle. It is even worth having two purses or wallets if you deal in cash – one for the housekeeping, and one for your own personal and business money.

You also have to remember that if you have a business partner, the financial affairs of the business are as much to do with that partner as they are to do with you, and a certain amount of confidentiality should be maintained. Discussing your business finances in detail with your domestic partner can lead to you discussing your business partner's personal finances with your domestic partner. This can be a tricky situation, and needs careful handling, particularly if your domestic partner has always been the one to handle the household finances.

WHAT YOU CAN CLAIM FOR TAX PURPOSES

Chapter 8 sets out in some detail what you can and cannot claim for tax purposes.

You might be able to claim for domestic cleaning services, if you work from home. Ask your accountant's advice on this, and make sure, before you claim, that your cleaner is declaring that income on his or her tax return.

PENSIONS

Women may or may not be entitled to a full state pension in their own right. If you have only ever paid a married woman's National Insurance stamp or have never paid any National Insurance at all, you will certainly not be entitled to draw your own pension; the cases of this are becoming rarer, because it is only women who are now in their late fifties and upwards who were entitled to take this option when they were earning.

You should certainly take out a pension in your own right if you possibly can. For one thing, the payments can be taken into account for tax purposes, and for another, you will ultimately be able to benefit yourself from your own business dealings. It will also give you the continued independence to which you have become accustomed.

Shop around for a pension which is best suited to your needs. Ask your accountant's advice, but be aware that some accountants are tied agents – that is, tied to one insurance company, which might not be the best for you. Try to find an independent accountant or insurance broker.

YOUR CAR EXPENSES

If you have been used to driving the family car, a car of your own can be an unexpectedly high expense. It is worth striving to get your own car through the business however, so that you are always independent and mobile.

Insight

If you run two or more vehicles, it's a good idea to organize the payment for insurance and tax at different times of the year, if possible. Otherwise all those bills come in at once, which could be at one of your quiet times.

The business will pay the tax, insurance, purchase and servicing costs, and these will be the same for a woman as for a man. However, if you have been driving the family car and it is insured in your domestic partner's name, you will have to start earning your own no claims bonus from the beginning. The no claims bonus usually belongs to the 'insured', the person the insurance companies reckon does the bulk of the driving. It does not matter if you have done the bulk of the driving, and have never made a claim – you will still have to start from scratch if you now become the insured. This can be an additional and unexpected expense. Some companies are now rectifying this.

CHECKLIST

Use this list to check your business and home circumstances:

▶ **At home:**
    ▷ *Which aspects of running my home are not well organized?*
    ▷ *Which chores do I do that other people could do or share?*
    ▷ *Are there any other labour-saving gadgets I could use?*
    ▷ *Can I afford someone to do the cleaning/gardening?*
    ▷ *Do I want someone to help in these areas?*

▶ **Children and other dependants:**
Which of these should I look into further?
    ▷ *Nannies*
    ▷ *Mother's or Father's help*
    ▷ *Childminders*
    ▷ *Home helps*
    ▷ *Meals on Wheels*
    ▷ *Home shopping services*
    ▷ *Child protection checks*

▶ **Health:**
    ▷ *Do I eat the right things?*
    ▷ *Do I eat at the right times?*
    ▷ *What regular exercise do I take?*
    ▷ *Do I have regular medical checkups?*

▶ **Image:**
    ▷ *What sort of image do I project?*
    ▷ *What else ought I to do?*

▶ **Money:**
    ▷ *Which aspects do I not understand?*
    ▷ *Where can I learn about those?*
    ▷ *Have I got a pension sorted out?*

Taking it further

You need not feel on your own when starting out in business, or when the time comes for expansion. There are numerous sources of help, support and advice, many of which are listed in this chapter.

Helpful sources of information: websites

ACAS (employment relations)   www.acas.org.uk

Advertising:
Yellow Pages   www.yell.com
Thomson   www.thomweb.co.uk

Advice:
Business Link   www.businesslink.gov.uk
Federation of Small   www.fsb.org.uk
  Businesses
The Prince's Trust   www.princes-trust.org.uk
Prime   www.primeinitiative.org.uk
A New Business   www.anewbusiness.co.uk
  (business names,
  trade marks, etc.)

Charities: HM Revenue & Customs Charities
tax reliefs and obligations   www.hmrc.gov.uk/charities/
                                index.htm

helpsheets   www.hmrc.gov.uk/charities/
                                leaflets.htm

The Charity Commission   www.charity-commission.gov.uk

Chartered Institute of   www.cipd.co.uk
  Personnel and Development

Commission for Racial Equality	www.cre.gov.uk
Companies Registration Office	www.companieshouse.gov.uk
Data Protection	www.dataprotection.gov.uk
Department for Business, Innovation & Skills	www.bis.gov.uk
Department of Work and Pensions	www.dwp.gov.uk
Employment rights: tailored interactive guidance	www.tiger.gov.uk
Equal Opportunities Commission	www.eoc.org.uk

Export:

The Institute of Export	www.export.org.uk
UK Trade and Investment	www.tradeinvest.gov.uk
SITPRO (Simplifying International Trade)	www.sitpro.org.uk

Franchising:

British Franchise Association	www.thebfa.org.uk
Health and Safety Executive	www.hse.gov.uk
Institute of Directors	www.iod.co.uk

Intellectual property:

UK Patent Office	www.patent.gov.uk
Learn Direct	www.learndirect.co.uk

Marketing:

The Chartered Institute of Marketing	www.cim.co.uk
Office of Fair Trading	www.oft.gov.uk

Pensions:
The Pensions Regulator   www.thepensionsregulator.gov.uk
Stakeholder Pensions   www.opra.gov.uk

Taxation and VAT:
HM Revenue & Customs   www.hmrc.gov.uk

Networking opportunities

Networking is an excellent way of exchanging ideas with
other local businesses and of promoting your own business.
The following may provide a starting point for some networking
ideas – see your local library for details:

- ▶ *Chamber of Commerce*
- ▶ *Rotary (for men)*
- ▶ *Women in Business Clubs (for women)*
- ▶ *Business and Professional Women (Tel: 020 7938 1729)*
- ▶ *Women in Management (Tel: 020 7382 9978)*
- ▶ *Breakfast clubs*
- ▶ *Federation of Small Businesses*

Learning opportunities

Your local Business Link will direct you to appropriate courses or
other learning opportunities. Business Links run free or subsidized
courses and seminars themselves and have details of local colleges
and training providers.

Typical Business Link courses and seminars are:

Information Technology, e.g. New User (Internet, Email, Windows);
Microsoft Office Applications (Excel, Outlook, PowerPoint, Word);
Building your website; Marketing your website.

Management, e.g. Management effectiveness; Motivating your
team; Conducting effective appraisal reviews; Success, planning

and delegation; Teambuilding and development; Recruiting, interviewing and selecting staff.

Health and Safety, e.g. First aid; Basic food hygiene.

Further reading

Many books for small businesses are available from bookshops, or from the library. The following is a small selection:

Get to Grips with Book keeping, Andrew Lymer and Nick Rowbottom (Hodder Headline)

Get Started in Franchising, Kurt Illetschko (Hodder Education)

Small Business Survival, Kevin Duncan (Hodder Education)

Make a Difference with Your Marketing, J. Jonathan Gabay (Hodder Education)

Run Your Own Business, Kevin Duncan (Hodder Education)

Get Started in Sage Line 50, MacBride (Hodder Headline)

Small Business Accounting, Andrew Lymer (Hodder Education)

Body Language, Allan Pease (Sheldon Press)

Book-keeping & Accounting for the Small Business, Peter Taylor (How To Books)

Buying your first Franchise, Greg Clarke (Daily Express/Kogan Page)

English Language Skills, Vera Hughes (Greenwich Exchange)

The 'Which?' Guide to Starting your own Business, (Which? Books)

The Right Way to Start your own Business, Rodney Willett (Elliot Right Way Books)

Running your own Business Made Easy, Roy Hedges (Lawpack Publishing)

Setting up and Running a Limited Company, Robert Browning (How To Books)

Start your Business Week by Week, Steve Parks (Pearson Education)

Starting your own Business, Jim Green (How To Books)

Index